CRUCIAL CONVERSATIONS ABOUT AMERICA'S SCHOOLS

John C. Draper and Nancy Protheroe

Because research and information make the difference.

Educational Research Service
1001 North Fairfax Street, Suite 500 • Alexandria, VA 22314
Phone: 703-243-2100 • Toll Free: 800-791-9308
Fax: 703-243-1985 • Toll Free: 800-791-9309

Because research and information make the difference.

Educational Research Service
1001 North Fairfax Street, Suite 500, Alexandria, VA 22314
Tel: 703-243-2100 or 800-791-9308
Fax: 703-243-1985 or 800-791-9309
Email: ers@ers.org • Web site: www.ers.org

Educational Research Service is *the* nonprofit organization providing school leaders with essential research for effective decisions. Founded by the national school management associations, ERS is the school leader's best source for resources and data to build more successful schools. Since 1973, education leaders have utilized the ERS advantage to make the most effective school decisions in both day-to-day operations and long-range planning. Refer to the last page of this publication to learn how you can benefit from the services and resources available through an annual ERS subscription. Or visit us online at www.ers.org for a more complete picture of the wealth of preK-12 research information and tools available through ERS subscriptions and resources.

Authors: Dr. John Draper and Nancy Protheroe
Editor: Tracy Pastian
Editorial Assistant: Alyssa Howell
Layout & Design: Susie McKinley and Libby McNulty

Ordering Information: Additional copies of *Crucial Conversations About America's Schools* may be purchased at the list price of $20.00; ERS School District Subscriber: $10.00; ERS Individual Subscriber: $15.00. Quantity discounts available. Add the greater of $4.50 or 10% of total purchase price for shipping and handling. Phone orders accepted with Visa, MasterCard, or American Express. Stock No. 0785. ISBN: 978-1-931762-97-7.

Table of Contents

Chapter 1:
Reshaping the Conversation About Public Schools

> "The skills required to master high-stakes interactions are quite easy to spot and moderately easy to learn." (Patterson, Grenny, McMillan, & Switzler, 2002, p. 25)

Public Schools Are Failing—Right?

The good news about public schools, for the most part, falls on deaf ears. But bad news often has a high profile. A prime example is found in a recent issue of *Newsweek* that focused on education and featured a lead article that began with a widely accepted—but unfounded—assertion: "The relative decline of American education at the elementary- and high-school levels has long been a national embarrassment as well as a threat to the nation's future." This sentence, unfortunately, embodies the perception of many citizens disconnected from our schools. As school leaders, we must acknowledge that perception, roll up our sleeves, and go to work on changing the mistaken belief that today's public schools are in the midst of a precipitous decline.

There are many reasons why this perception persists, but they are fodder for another book. This book is not about the "why" behind the belief. Instead, it is about stopping the actions of educators that unintentionally feed it by not being aggressive enough in providing a more accurate and comprehensive picture of our schools. It is about helping school leaders understand the "how" of promoting crucial conversations about public schools.

In his book, *Sixteen Trends*, Gary Marx shares his thoughts on the responsibility of educational leaders.

> Effective leaders understand the need to bring others on board. Leaders connect people and ideas. They bring them together in common purpose and build a sense of ownership. They tap the richness of thinking that is already there in schools, colleges, and other organizations, and in the community. When people are engaged, they're more likely to declare, "We're all in this together." (2006)

He is on target for the message we need to use to counter misperceptions of public schools. We are all in this together—and school leaders must help citizens across the nation realize that, in general, public schools are working better than ever before and working for the good of all. For many of our citizens, this will represent a massive paradigm shift that will require information to be presented in a different way. The goal is helping these people better understand our schools so they can better believe in, care about, and support them.

As you read the example of a classic paradigm shift on p. 3, apply it to the current plight of school educators trying to meet the disparate challenges of excellence and equity with an increasingly unsupportive public unaware of the rocky urban myth of failing public schools.

Example of a Classic Paradigm Shift

"Two battleships assigned to the training squadron had been at sea on maneuvers in heavy weather for several days. I was serving on the lead battleship and was on watch on the bridge as night fell. The visibility was poor with patchy fog, so the captain remained on the bridge keeping an eye on all activities.

Shortly after dark, the lookout on the wing of the bridge reported, 'Light, bearing on the starboard bow.'

'Is it steady or moving astern?' the captain called out.

Lookout replied, 'Steady, captain,' which meant we were on a collision course with that ship.

The captain then called to the signalman, 'Signal that ship: We are on a collision course, advise you change course 20 degrees.'

Back came a signal, 'Advisable for you to change course 20 degrees.'

The captain said, 'Send, I'm a captain, change course 20 degrees.'

'I'm a seaman second class,' came the reply. 'You had better change course 20 degrees.'

By that time, the captain was furious. He spat out, 'Send, I'm a battleship. Change course 20 degrees.'

Back came the flashing light, 'I'm a lighthouse.'

We changed course."

Source: Covey, 1989, p. 33. Attributed to Frank Koch in the Naval Institute magazine, *Proceedings*.

At times we try to help someone and our efforts are rebuffed or even create hostility. This often happens when we challenge others' beliefs. That's why educators must create paradigm shifts—changes in the way someone thinks based on new information and understanding (see Covey, 1989, for more information). Facts or information can make a difference, but facts alone have not turned the tide in the crucial conversations about public schools. It is up to school leaders to more effectively engage communities in the crucial conversations necessary to help citizens appreciate the positive impact of our schools and avoid the rocks that threaten our national ship of education.

Most school leaders choose their vocation not out of a desire to work with the media, adults, or public opinion. They choose education because they love teaching and learning. They are highly motivated to see children succeed. Many don't particularly like engaging in politics; however, today's school leaders must take on this challenging, essential role.

School leaders must be the voice of their students, because their students don't have a vote. No longer do school leaders have the luxury of focusing on students and staff as their only responsibilities. School leaders need to look beyond the school building and actively build the connections necessary to change the perceptions, misconceptions, and myths about our schools.

Unfortunately, those who continually cite a "crisis" in public schools in order to advance their political or other agenda are rarely challenged. In *Education Hell: Rhetoric vs. Reality,* Gerald Bracey (2009) tells of the misleading Presidential Commission report published in 1983 titled *A Nation at Risk*. The report used inflammatory language such as "being overtaken by competitors throughout the world," "a rising tide of mediocrity," and "if an unfriendly foreign power had attempted to impose the mediocre education performance that exists today, we might well have viewed it as an act of war" to advance a political agenda (in Bracey, 2009, p. 54). After the report was published, Ronald Reagan thanked the commissioners for their support of school prayer, vouchers, and their recommendation to eliminate the U. S. Department of Education—none of which was mentioned in the report. The commission did review National Assessment of Educational Progress (NAEP) scores for 9-, 13-, and 17-year-olds in reading, math, and science. Scores were up in reading and math for all three groups. They were up in two of the groups for science. The only declining trend was among 17-year-olds in science—and that was the only trend line used by the commission (Bracey, 2009).

Why doesn't the truth about such contrived crises in public education dispel the rumors? In *Made to Stick,* authors Chip and Dan Heath (2007) explore what makes an urban myth "stick." Urban myths such as razor blades in Halloween candy, seeing the Great Wall of China from space, and fried rats in Kentucky Fried Chicken stick because they are memorable, concrete, unexpected stories. Once you hear them, you remember them. Statistics, hard-to-understand language, and unemotional information do not stick and will not change the way people think or believe (Heath & Heath, 2007). The best way to unstick an urban myth is to make the truth "stickier." By paying attention to this simple axiom, school leaders will be better prepared to share the good news about public schools in a way that works.

Patterson et al. ask: What makes a conversation crucial "as opposed to plain vanilla" (2002, p. 1)? In their view, crucial conversations have three characteristics. First, the people involved in the conversation have differing opinions on an issue. Second, stakes are high. Third, emotions are strong—sometimes "really strong." By definition, they "are about tough issues" (p. 2) and, thus, so potentially risky that it might seem reasonable to avoid them whenever possible.

Public Perception of Public Schools

For several decades, the annual Phi Delta Kappa (PDK) poll has recorded the opinions of the public on public school issues. In the 2009 poll, 74% of parents of school-age children gave their oldest child's school a grade of A or B. When citizens were asked to grade local public schools, 51% gave a grade of A or B. When asked to grade public schools in the nation as a whole, only 19% gave a grade of A or B (1% an A and 18% a B). This has been a consistent finding in PDK/Gallup polls. Most people like their local schools—particularly if they actually have a child attending the school—but think badly about the schools "out there."

Local school leaders might ask, "So what's the problem? My community thinks our schools are pretty good!" The problem is that there are always more people "out there" than there are at home—and they think your schools are lousy. Educators know that differences in schools and districts are highly dependent on the demographics of the different communities. Thus, "quality" comparisons are often misleading. But educators sometimes present data about their own schools in a way that reflects poorly on a neighboring school or district. Although this is not intentional, such comparisons that cast another district or school in a poor light contribute to the myth about the nation's "failing" schools.

The TLC Formula for School Leaders

What should a school leader do to shift public perceptions about schools in general from dissatisfaction to a better understanding of what public education actually does for our country and its children? To start, begin internalizing this thought: *The greatest power you have as a leader is to establish the conversation.* Conversations make a difference and are the first—and potentially most powerful—step toward increasing understanding about and support for our schools. Use these three guidelines—the TLC's of effective conversations—to frame your work:

1. **T**hink about and talk about what you believe and why you believe it.
2. **L**earn to use language that reframes the challenges and issues of public schools.
3. **C**onnect your community to your students using *stories* that bridge the gaps between generations, classes, races, and religions.

In the 2008 PDK/Gallup Poll, prior to the election, respondents were asked "Who should the new President rely on most for advice on education policy?" In a refreshing result, only 4% selected political leaders and only 14% chose business leaders. An overwhelming **77% selected educational leaders as the most reliable source for advice!** It is reassuring that Americans want school leaders to step up and speak out on what is best for public schools. However, this begs a question—are the voices of educational leaders being heard?

Sadly, they may not be. Take a look at this quote from President Barack Obama, whom most consider to be strongly supportive of public education: "Despite resources that are unmatched anywhere in the world, we've let our grades slip, our schools crumble, our teacher quality fall short, and other nations outpace us" (in Strauss, 2009). Thus, it's clear that the myth of widespread failure by our schools extends all the way to the top and that these negative perceptions don't come only from naysayers of public schools. The bottom line is that school leaders are not connecting in a way that resonates with the people and our national leaders.

> The greatest power you have as a leader is to establish the conversation.

In the following chapters of this book we will focus on five issues facing public education and the conversations that educators and communities could be having about them. Obviously it is important to be knowledgeable when you engage in the crucial conversations surrounding public schools, but, more importantly, you must also be able to deliver your message effectively. This opening chapter will help you build the know-how to lead those effective conversations.

1. Think about and talk about what you believe and why you believe it.

As educators, we have an innate, shared value system that we rarely put into words. We often incorrectly assume that others understand and share the same values. Doesn't everyone want every child to succeed and to be healthy, happy, and productive? Most do, but their frame of reference about the role public education plays in meeting those goals may be different from ours. Those who think badly about public schools are not stupid, they are not unpatriotic, and they are not mean, greedy, or uncaring towards children. They may be uninformed and/or fearful of change, but they are not the enemy of school leaders. The enemies are ignorance and separation, and the paths to victory over these enemies are education and mutuality[1]. Recognizing this, school leaders must be proactive in building connections to offset the separation within our society in order to preserve public schools.

School leaders must begin by articulating what they believe and why. In the words of a country song by Aaron Tippin (Tippin & Brock, 1990), "You've got to stand for something or you'll fall for anything." Heartfelt words make a difference when they are both spoken and heard. Be reassured and confident that your values as an educator are the very best of traditional American values. Put them into words. Do you believe that public education is the backbone of democracy? Say so! Thomas Jefferson did: *"If a nation expects to be ignorant and free . . . it expects what never was and will never be."*

1 Mutuality—a reciprocal relation between interdependent entities. As used here, it implies an understanding of the shared values between different subgroups of the public.

Do you believe that it is the responsibility of each of us to provide for the education of all of us? Say so! Abraham Lincoln did: *"Upon the subject of education . . . I can only say that I view it as the most important subject which we as a people can be engaged in."*

Do you believe that every child deserves a quality education regardless of where she lives or who her parents are? Say so! Do you believe that, while standardized tests can provide some measurement of student achievement, qualities such as creativity, self-discipline, curiosity, persistence, courage, imagination, enthusiasm, and patriotism are equally important? Say so!

Do you believe that the purpose of our schools is *not* to fill the minds of students with facts, but to teach them how to think? Say so! Do you believe that all children can learn and that all children are born with different gifts and abilities? Say so! (As a middle school principal, I used to tell parents that all children were gifted—some academically, some athletically, and some socially. Parents of overly talkative seventh-graders have ruefully shared with me during disciplinary conferences that their child was the socially gifted one.)

It is important to think about and talk about where you stand and why you stand there. It's also important to do so with respect and consideration. As educators, we know it is foolish to be angry at a child because he's ignorant of something. Anyone can see the foolishness in being angry at a handicapped child in a wheelchair because he won't get up and walk. Similarly, it is counterproductive to be mad at those who think differently than we do. Those who think differently need to see school leaders modeling respect and dignity. Listen carefully and sincerely to those who disagree with you. You may not agree with what they say, but basic values for educators should include a respect for ideas and a quest for knowledge. You cannot influence others unless you are open to being influenced! The Bill of Rights guarantees that we are free to have different opinions and beliefs and that our right to do so is protected. Diversity is a fundamental principle in our Constitution, and it should be a fundamental part of leading the crucial conversations about public schools.

An old adage says that teachers teach three ways: by example, by example, and by example. The same is true for school leaders. The lessons we teach by remaining calm, reasoned, and respectful when engaged in crucial conversations with others are important. It should be clear in our discussions that we love this country, we care about the nation's school children, and we want a positive outcome for all citizens.

The *How* of Dialogue

- "Start with heart. That is, your own heart. If you can't get yourself right, you'll have a hard time getting dialogue right" (Patterson et al., 2002, pp. 27-28).
- Keep an eye on the *conditions* of the conversation as well as content. "By watching for the moment a conversation starts turning unhealthy, you can respond quickly. The sooner you catch a problem, the sooner you'll be able to work your way back to healthy dialogue, and the less severe the damage" (Patterson et al., 2002, p. 461).
- Make it safe. If you spot safety risks, step out of the conversation, shift toward safter footing by building in the elements of mutual purpose and mutual respect, and then step back in.

The belief that America's public schools are failing will not be changed quickly. It will take diligence and dedication on the part of educators. There is no quick fix or silver bullet to magically change the way the majority of citizens feel about our schools. That's ok. As educators, we know that the lessons we teach may take months, years, or even decades to come to fruition in our students. Bring that same patience, respect, and dignity to the crucial conversations about schools.

2. Learn to use language that reframes the challenges and issues of public schools.

Language is important. As school leaders, we should not use language that is at odds with our beliefs. We must develop and use language that communicates our paradigm. Stephen Covey (1989) explains a paradigm as "the lens through which we see the world," and George Lakoff (2004) takes it a step further, saying, "Once your frame is accepted into the discourse, everything you say is just common sense."

Some people honestly perceive public schools as the enemy. They use language that conjures up a negative impression without actually addressing the reality of public schools. Some choose to substitute the phrase "government schools" for "public schools." A few go on to miscategorize public schools as "Godless"—resulting in "Godless, government schools." Notice how easily the phrase rolls off your tongue using alliteration. "Godless, government schools" is a damaging label for the schools in which we work. I know of no educator who, when asked where he or she works, would respond with "in a Godless, government school." It is not a true representation of our schools.

The language grows even more damaging by adding "Godless, government schools *staffed with selfish union employees.*" The selfish union employee label falsely paints teachers as interested only in increased salary and benefits while the union protects their mediocrity and lack of performance. There may be a few bad apples in the bunch, but almost all teachers want to do a good job and they care about kids. Public schools welcome all children into their classrooms. America's schools feed lunch and breakfast to countless hungry children every school day. Children from dysfunctional families find safety and support within those school walls. Miracles happen every day in public schools.

How to Reframe a Conversation

- Be sincere. Use frames you really believe in, based on values you really hold.
- Avoid the usual mistakes. Remember, don't just negate the other person's claims; reframe. The unframed facts will not set you free. You cannot win just by stating the true facts and showing that they contradict your opponent's claims. Frames trump facts. His frames will stay and the facts will bounce off. Always reframe. If you remember nothing else about framing, remember this: *Once your frame is accepted into the discourse, everything you say is just common sense.* Why? Because that's what common sense is: reasoning within a commonplace, accepted frame.
- Never answer a question framed from your opponent's point of view. Always reframe the question to fit your values and your frames. Practice changing frames.
- Tell a story. Find stories where your frame is built into the story. Build up a stock of effective stories.

Source: Lakoff, 2004.

More damaging language occurs when the sentence is completed: "Godless, government schools staffed with selfish, union employees *leaving little children behind.*" Now that the No Child Left Behind Act (NCLB) is labeling schools across the nation as failing, some falsely think that public schools are in the business of leaving children behind. "No child left behind" is a wonderful **goal** that should be embraced by every school leader—but it is a terrible **measure** of success. Schools are assessed primarily by what they fail to do. It is as unfair as giving a zero to a student who missed one question out of 100 on a test. Parents and students would, understandably, be livid. That scoring methodology has left many schools with an undeserved black eye. Unfortunately, that is the image some have of public schools.

School leaders must change this frame of reference. Educators need to develop the skills required to move to the frame or paradigm that accurately and positively describes the reality of our schools. For example, use the phrase "*caring, community schools*" to more correctly identify schools. Every school is a reflection of the community in which it is found, and even struggling schools are staffed with many educators who care deeply about their students.

If you ask a teacher where she works, the answer of "in a caring, community school" is the frame we want every teacher and staff member to hold. *Caring, community schools* are what we want for every district. The children within a caring, community school are the responsibility of the entire community. The phrase invites support and engagement. Caring, community schools rise to the challenge of providing for all children. Caring, community schools are an asset to the district and an investment in the future. I have seen numerous examples of this caring. One example immediately comes to mind—so often, when the home of a family in the community burns, public schools have wrapped their arms of support around the children within hours. It is not unusual to have clothes, school supplies, food, and shelter organized by the school and its PTA before the ashes of the burned home have cooled.

"Caring community schools *staffed with sincere, dedicated professionals"* adds to the paradigm. We all know from personal experience how important the teacher is to the learning process. Many teachers feel a "calling" to work in education. Daniel Pink (2009) explores the growing awareness of how important intrinsic rewards are to motivation (and how rewards contingent on performance can actually decrease motivation—a sobering thought to supporters of performance-based pay). Teachers and others who work in education have been acutely aware for decades that the rewards of the profession are frequently nonmonetary.

"Caring community schools staffed with sincere, dedicated professionals *providing every child with every chance for success"* completes the paradigm. While educators chafe at the impossibility of ensuring that every child will be successful, they should welcome the accountability of providing every child with every chance for success. As mentioned earlier, leaving no child behind is an admirable goal, but not an adequate measure of school effectiveness. But although student success is not something that can be guaranteed, educators can be held accountable for giving every child every chance every day. Educators must not waiver in the commitment to give every child every chance.

Caring, community schools staffed with sincere, dedicated professionals providing every child every chance for success. That is the frame that school leaders should use in the crucial conversations about public schools.

3. Connect your community to your students using *stories* that bridge the gap between generations, classes, races, and religions.

Educators have the "curse of knowledge." It's a phrase used by Chip and Dan Heath (2007) and it refers to the difficulty of thinking **as if you did not know what you already know**. You don't know what it is like not to know what you know. Read this sentence: We need an IEP for that new, ADHD, LD student. If you know what it means, you have the education curse of knowledge.

Unfortunately for school leaders, the years of study and preparation for your career work against you when you are communicating with those outside education. The university classes and conferences where you spent countless hours learning the vocabulary of your trade can now handicap your effectiveness.

Using Stories to Convey Your Message

"Every time you try to convince others through verbal persuasion, you suffer from your inability to select and share language in a way that reproduces in the mind of the listener exactly the same thoughts you are having. You say *your* words, but others hear *their* words, which in turn stimulates *their* images, *their* past histories, and *their* overall meaning—all of which may be very different from what you intended... Effective stories... overcome this. A well-told narrative provides concrete and vivid detail... It changes people's view of how the world works because it presents a plausible, touching, and memorable flow of cause and effect that can alter people's view of the consequences of various actions or beliefs." (Patterson et al., 2008, pp. 58-59)

Anyone who has sat through a boring lecture knows that facts and information are remarkably forgettable. We have all had teachers in our past who relied solely on lecture and offered little in the way of student engagement. However, there are also teachers in our past whose lessons we still remember years later. What makes their teaching so sticky? How can we make the truths about our schools that sticky? And, just as important, how do we "unstick" a misconception that is damaging to public schools?

Public schools are a huge operation organized and funded by every state and they employ millions of people nationwide. They are labor-intensive and expensive. It is difficult to justify the expense if you approach public schools as a service industry for students. It is uninspiring. To justify it, we must appeal to the top of Maslow's ladder. Originally presented as a ladder of needs, from physical to security all the way up to learning and transcendence (helping others realize their potential), psychology textbooks now recognize the needs but not necessarily the hierarchy. It seems that people pursue all these needs simultaneously. Most people claim to be motivated by the "higher" rungs on Maslow's ladder such as learning and self-fulfillment, but, in a surprising twist, assume that others are primarily motivated by physical and security needs (Heath & Heath, 2007).

If school leaders want others to support public schools, they must appeal to the "higher good." Education must be viewed in its broader sense. Gilbert Chesterton once said, "Education is simply the soul of a society as it passes from one generation to another." Henry Ford said, "Anyone who stops learning is old, whether at twenty or eighty. Anyone who keeps learning stays young." It is too easy to mistake the daily tasks of teaching, transporting, feeding and managing students as just work. **Teaching is a job—but saving lives through education is a mission**. The mission is what motivates, not the routine.

The challenge is to connect others to the mission of public education. We do it by personalizing the message. When school leaders talk about students, teachers, or support workers as a group, we lose the mission. Charities know that it is more effective to tell the story of one starving child and ask for a donation than to tell about 10,000 nameless, starving children in a third-world country. Similarly, a story that features the success of one student, the caring of one particular teacher, or the dedication of one specific support employee is more effective in building support for the whole district.

Stories stick because they overcome the educational curse of knowledge. The story is more powerful than the message. You can't always remember the story from the message, but you can always get the message from the story. In addition, stating a position or policy invites the listener to evaluate and judge what is said. Telling a story actually engages the listener in the experience. It effectively short-circuits the negativity that the listener may be carrying and goes straight to the hearer's heart. If you want them to remember what you say, tell a true story with a message, and provide—but don't focus on—the facts.

When we share the story of the public school teacher who donates a kidney to a student, perceptions about teachers begin to change. When we share the story of the coach who took one of his athletes from a poor family to the department store and bought the boy his first sport coat to wear to the athletic banquet, perceptions begin to change. When we share the story of the school bus driver who provides books for her students to read on the bus, perceptions began to change. When we share the story about the janitor who takes a special education student under his wing and helps him learn a trade, perceptions begin to change. When we share the story about the basketball player with Down syndrome who finally gets in the game and *both teams* work to help him score a goal, perceptions begin to change.

Heath and Heath (2007, pp. 226-229) identify two of the best stories for motivating us to act and changing perception as:

- **Challenge Plot** stories—David and Goliath is the classic Challenge Plot story. These stories motivate and inspire us. They are about dedication, perseverance, overcoming obstacles, victory by the underdog, and triumph of good over evil. Think of the Alamo, Rosa Parks, Valley Forge, Seabiscuit, *Star Wars*, and so on. These stories make us want to work harder, take on new challenges, overcome adversity. Challenge Plot stories drawn from our schools are effective with those outside public education because they repaint the incorrect pictures some carry about pubic school employees. Challenge Plot stories can erase ignorance about those who work in public schools. (These stories can be, by the way, very effective with your own employees. If you want to keep your teachers motivated and engaged, pepper your conversation with Challenge Plot stories.)

- **Connection Plot** stories—The story of the Good Samaritan is a classic Connection Plot. Today, being a "good Samaritan" means voluntarily helping others in distress, but the story of the Good Samaritan as it was written in the Bible had deeper meaning for the original hearers because of their prejudice against the Samaritan people. In the original context, the Samaritan was a not just a nice guy, he was a nice guy who stepped across cultural barriers to help someone. These stories are about bridging the barriers of race, class, culture, religion, or demographics. Think Romeo and Juliet, *Three Cups of Tea,* and *The Blind Side.* These stories make us want to help others, work with others, care about others, and be more understanding of others. They can be used to connect facets of our community with students in our schools who are of a different age, color, social class, or religion than they are. Connection Plot stories help your community members discover the mutuality they share with your students.

Fortunately, you don't have to make up these stories. They surround us. School leaders just have to learn the art of "story spotting." Bob Ocwieja is not particularly famous, but the story he spotted is one you'll know (Heath & Heath, 2007). He was a Subway franchise owner in Chicago who heard about an obese college student who ate small, healthy sandwiches each day at a Subway in Bloomington, Illinois, and lost a lot of weight. Ocwieja brought the story to the attention of a local Subway ad manager and the rest is history. The first ad with Jared ran on January 1, 2000. It was simply Jared, who weighed only 185 lbs., standing in front of his home and holding a pair of the pants that he wore when he weighed 425 lbs.! The next day, *USA Today*, ABC, and Fox News called. On the third day, Oprah called and invited Jared to be a guest on her show. You could say the message stuck! Today it's a classic Challenge Plot story. We remember Jared, but not Bob Ocwieja. Bob just had to keep his eyes and ears open for stories that would resonate with the public—and that's what school leaders must do as well.

You don't need to be a talented speaker to be effective. Have your research and information, but don't use it unless requested. Using it simply to demonstrate to your audience—whether it's one person or a packed auditorium—that you have the issues under control will weaken your message. If your time is short, just tell the Connection Plot story that will resonate with your hearers and help them care about your students, their success, and the mission of your district.

The Simple Solution for Separation

There is no easy way to dispel the belief that America's public schools are failing, but we can tell our success stories and begin to change the perception. There are opportunists who use the politics of fear and division to capitalize on ignorance and separation for personal gain (Glass, 2008). School leaders must realize that the best counter to ignorance and separation is education and mutuality. Education and the discovery of mutuality dispel ignorance and overcome separation.

One of the best methods of changing the myth surrounding public schools is simply connecting your students to the community.

Educators have always encouraged parents and community members to visit schools. Community involvement is part of the plan for successful schools. Now it is time to take another step. With an ever-increasing percentage of adults who have no school-age children, we must do more than invite community members to sponsor or attend school events. School leaders must proactively connect students with the community. *It is no longer enough to invite outsiders in, school leaders must take their students out into the community.*

When we interact and have common experiences, we quickly discover that fear and distrust are unfounded. Organize field trips for your second-graders to sing at the local senior citizens home. The students will have fun and the senior citizens will learn that little boys and girls who may look different than them are still just kids and nothing to fear. Have your sixth-graders interview an elderly neighbor in the community and write a paper on how things have changed since 1960 and, in the process, the neighbor will begin to realize how much children are still the same. Set up a plan for your high school freshmen to research local businesses and business leaders and the leaders will begin to take ownership in the success of the school. Let your student council organize a student mock court, city council, or county commission meeting *in the actual chambers* with community leaders present and the leaders will have a new appreciation for the abilities of the students.

Seek out every opportunity to mix your students with adults who may have forgotten how important public education is to the community and the nation. Constantly interject your beliefs and why you believe that schools are important, such as:

- If students get a good education, they are more likely to become productive members of society.
- Healthy communities need strong public schools.
- Most Americans who have worked their way out of poverty attended public schools.
- Better educated than incarcerated.
- Public schools are the engine of opportunity for all Americans.

During all of this, school leaders must tell the stories that inspire, uplift, motivate, and connect us as a country. America needs some TLC, and public school leaders are the ones who must deliver it. Let's look at the TLC's of crucial conversations again:

1. **T**hink about and talk about what you believe and why you believe it
2. **L**earn to use language that reframes the challenges and issues of public schools
3. **C**onnect your community to your students using *stories* that bridge the gap between generations, classes, races, and religions

The TLC of conversations applies to all the groups school leaders need to reach. Many times, the conversations need to begin with employees and parents. Those audiences should be the most engaged and the most supportive of public schools. Simultaneously, conversations with elected officials, community leaders, business leaders, and adults with no school-age children must also occur. The principles of TLC will still apply.

The next chapters of this book focus on five of the many topics—typically presented negatively—that are swirling about public schools today. Most of the five selected topics are driven by Race to the Top funding and other positions emanating from the Department of Education. The topic summaries that follow are, by necessity, fairly brief. They address the issues from three perspectives:

1. What is the "talk" about the issue?
2. What is the "truth" based on current research? (Remember, the point in crucial conversations isn't to drown people in facts, but it is important to have a solid, research-based understanding of the issue.)
3. What is the "crucial conversation" (the core questions) that school leaders need to address?

Though this book focuses on only five issues, there are many other valid topics deserving of crucial conversations, such as school safety, international competition, teaching to the test, and the teaching of character in our schools. All these crucial conversations can be most effectively broached using the TLC of conversations. Be respectful, be positive, and persevere.

> "What the best and wisest parent wants for his own child, that must the community want for all of its children. Any other ideal for our schools is narrow and unlovely; acted upon it destroys our democracy." — John Dewey

References

Bracey, G. W. (2009). *Education hell: Rhetoric vs. reality: Transforming the fire consuming America's schools.* Alexandria, VA: Educational Research Service.

Covey, S. R. (1989). *The 7 habits of highly effective people: Powerful lessons in personal change.* New York: Fireside.

Glass, G. V. (2008). *Fertilizers, pills, and magnetic strips: The fate of public education in America.* Charlotte, NC: Information Age Publishing.

Heath, C., & Heath, D. (2007). *Made to stick: Why some ideas survive and others die.* New York: Random House.

Lakoff, G. (2004). *Don't think of an elephant! Know your values and frame the debate.* White River Junction, VT: Chelsea Green Publishing.

Marx, G. (2006). *Sixteen trends: Their profound impact on our future: Implications for students, education, communities, and the whole of society.* Arlington, VA: Educational Research Service.

Patterson, K., Grenny, J., McMillan, R., & Switzler, A. (2002). *Crucial conversations: Tools for talking when the stakes are high.* New York: McGraw-Hill.

PDK/Gallup Poll. (2008). *PDK/Gallup poll of the public's attitudes toward the public schools.*

PDK/Gallup Poll. (2009). *PDK/Gallup poll of the public's attitudes toward the public schools.* Retrieved from Phi Delta Kappa, http://www.pdkintl.org/kappan/poll.htm.

Pink, D. H. (2009). *Drive: The surprising truth about what motivates us.* New York: Riverhead Books.

Thomas, E., & Wingert, P. (2010, March 15). Why we must fire bad teachers. *Newsweek.*

Strauss, V. (2009, March 16). Putting some straight talk into Obama's education speech. *The Washington Post.* Retrieved from http://www.washingtonpost.com/wp-dyn/content/article/2009/03/15/AR2009031502068.html?sid=ST2009031603074

Tippin, A., & Brock, B. (1990). You've got to stand for something [Recorded by A Tippin]. On *You've got to stand for something.* Nashville, TN: RCA.

Chapter 2:
The Dropout Rate

The Talk

Too many of our high schools are dropout factories, and we're not making enough progress in addressing this critical problem.

The Truth

Dropout rates *are* unacceptably high and at crisis proportions in some schools. But these schools are in the minority. In addition, districts and schools across the country—even those with low dropout rates—have begun to more aggressively address the problem.

There are some easy points of agreement. We all know that dropping out of school limits opportunities for too many of our youngsters, with lifelong ramifications for them as well as for our country. The Alliance for Excellent Education (2008) estimates that almost 7,000 students drop out each school day. At the current rate, there will be more than 13 million students who drop out of high school over the next decade (Alliance for Excellent Education, 2010). The data also point to even more troubling concerns. Dropout rates are much higher for Black and Latino students, as well as for students coming from low-income homes.

According to the Alliance for Excellent Education, while "78 percent of white students graduate from high school on time with a regular diploma, only about 55 percent of African American and 58 percent of Hispanics do so" (2008, p. 1).

We also have too many schools with dropout rates of 50% or more. Balfanz and Legters estimate that there are "between 900 and 1,000 high schools in which surviving to the senior year is at best a 50/50 proposition" (2004, p. 60). Since many—although not all—of these are large, urban high schools, the U.S. Department of Education estimates that half the nation's dropouts are products of 2,000 high schools.

But this bleak picture is starting to turn around. A 2009 study conducted by researchers at Johns Hopkins University analyzed data from every state to attempt to get a handle on the dropout problem—and to assess whether progress is being made in addressing it. While they found that the overall graduation rate remained essentially flat from 2002 to 2006, 18 states posted gains and, "in 12 states which can serve as models for the nation, the gains were substantial" (Balfanz & West, 2009, p. iii). In 2006, four states were within striking distance of achieving the target of 90% graduation rate, and at least 19 states had graduation rates of 80% or higher.

Balfanz and West also studied schools from the perspective of their "promoting power"—specifically, a comparison of the students enrolled in 12th grade to the number enrolled 4 years earlier in 9th grade (3 years earlier for high schools comprised of grades 10-12). While not focusing on the number of students who actually graduate, promoting power can more easily be calculated for every school in the country and provides an indicator of the proportion of students on track to graduate. Some good news trends were identified in this area also. Specifically, progress is being made across the country in efforts to increase the number of schools with high promoting power. Some states have also made notable progress in decreasing the number of schools with weak promoting power and have made significant improvements in the percentage of minority students attending high promoting power schools rather than low promoting power schools.

Crucial Conversations

It's time for the conversation to shift from simply recognizing the problem and placing blame to talking about ways to put strategies in place that decrease the number of students who leave school before graduating. A positive side benefit of the intense interest in the dropout problem has been an effort by educators, policy makers, and researchers to identify approaches that can make a difference—and that should be the focus of the conversations about the dropout problem. We'll look briefly at a few of these approaches:

- Review district/school policies and practices that may be "encouraging" students to drop out.
- Ask students what might make a difference.
- Focus on early identification of potential dropouts and provide interventions to address students' unique needs.
- Provide multiple graduation options.
- Include the broader community in efforts to address the dropout problem.

Review District/School Policies and Practices That May Be "Encouraging" Students to Drop Out

Balfanz, Fox, Bridgeland, and McNaught ask: "Are there policies and practices that need to be changed?" Discussing these—at both the district and school levels—and making changes where appropriate can increase the likelihood that students will stay in school through graduation. They go on to discuss some of the types of policies that should be reviewed:

> A wide range of what may be viewed as customary, benign or even important individual school and district-wide policies and practices can inadvertently encourage, enable or fail to prevent dropping out. These include:
>
> Attendance policies. In some districts, no formal response to student absence is required until students miss a certain number of consecutive days (e.g., five) or a total number of days (e.g., 10). This tells schools it is okay to do nothing until it is almost too late. It also leads some students to become expert manipulators of the system, always missing one day short of a mandatory response. A better policy demands that every absence have a response. Schools need to have accurate lists of who is in school and who is not and mechanisms to reach parents and students.
>
> Grade retention policies. Social promotion does not work, but neither does holding students back, especially once they reach adolescence. When secondary students are held back, they often become dropouts.... It is much more effective to use extended school days, Saturdays, and summer school to enable students to catch up than to hold them back.

Grade promotion policies. In some districts, if students do not earn enough credits to be promoted from a grade, they must repeat the entire grade—retaking classes they already passed. Students should be required to retake only the classes they have failed and should receive supports so they can rejoin their peers mid-year or earlier.

Grading policies. In some districts, students are graded on a scale from 0 to 100, and students receive 0s when they do not turn in assignments or they miss exams. This can make it nearly impossible for students to recover. A single 0, averaged with an 80, averages to a failing grade of 40. Even an additional 100 only moves the grade to a still-failing 60! Other districts set the floor of their scale at 60. This enables students to receive a failing grade, if appropriate, but it also allows them to recover and pass the course if their effort and grades improve. Another grading policy that can encourage students to work hard to improve is a "B or better" policy. With this policy, the only acceptable grade for major projects, papers, and tests is a B, because research shows that students who receive Bs and As in high school succeed in college. Students redo assignments or retake tests until they achieve a B or better; then the second grade is averaged with their initial grade to produce a final grade. (Balfanz, Fox, et al., 2009, pp. 35-36)

"Schools vary in their ability to get students on track, and graduate those that fall off track" (MetisNet, 2008, p. 14).

Ask Students What Might Make a Difference

Asking young people in your school or district—both those still in school and those who dropped out—what school-related factors might encourage them to stay in school can provide a valuable resource. Some research projects have taken this approach. In one of these (Bridgeland, DiIulio, & Morison, 2006), focus groups and interviews with dropouts aged 16-25 identified some key areas that schools and districts should address in their dropout prevention efforts (see Table 2.1). Four of every five of these young people said that it would have made a difference to them if classes had been more in line with their personal interests and had a more direct connection between school and work. Over half saw the need for better supports for struggling students. They also stressed the need to strengthen the focus on academics, with more structure in place both for individual students and classrooms in general. They felt that a key to keeping students in school was better communication between home and school and increased parental/family involvement. Finally, they stressed the importance of individual student-adult relationships:

> These young people craved one-on-one attention from their teachers, and when they received it, they remembered it making a difference. Participants in the focus groups recounted that some of their best days were when their teachers noticed them, got them involved in class, and told them they were doing well. (Bridgeland, DiIulio, & Morison, 2006, p. 13)

> Ensuring that more students graduate requires a commitment to a series of manageable, focused, actionable steps—starting with understanding whether your students are progressing, which students are off track, and why they fall off track. Data tools help create an early warning system to determine which groups of students are more likely to drop out, the size of those groups, and the names of the students in those groups. (Bill & Melinda Gates Foundation, 2010, p. 4)

Improve Students' Chances

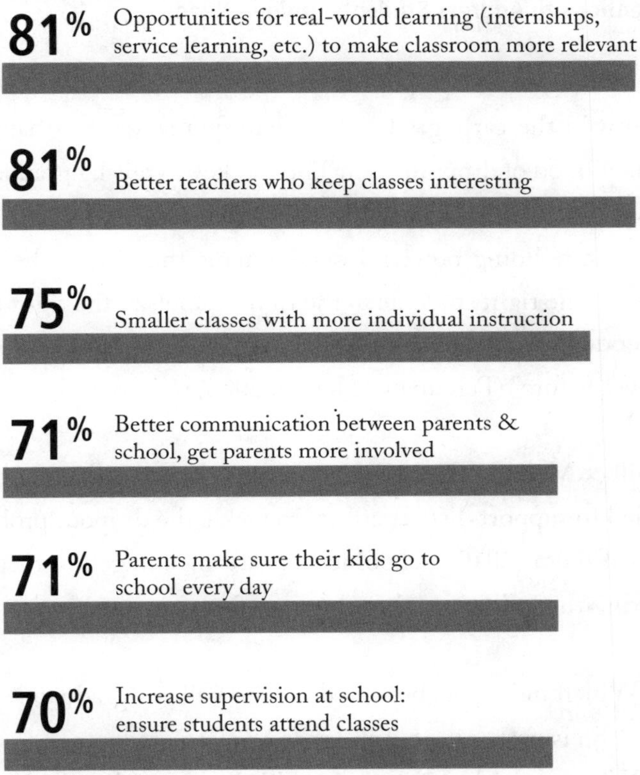

81% Opportunities for real-world learning (internships, service learning, etc.) to make classroom more relevant

81% Better teachers who keep classes interesting

75% Smaller classes with more individual instruction

71% Better communication between parents & school, get parents more involved

71% Parents make sure their kids go to school every day

70% Increase supervision at school: ensure students attend classes

Source: Bridgeland, J. M., DiIulio, J. J., & Morison, K. B. (2006). *The silent epidemic: Perspectives of high school dropouts*. Civic Enterprises, LLC. Used with permission.

Focus on Early Identification of Potential Dropouts and Provide Interventions to Address Students' Unique Needs

A key finding of the dropout research points to indicators available even in the early grades that identify a student as having a high likelihood of dropping out. Thus, a "key to raising graduation rates lies not just in identifying the best intervention strategies, but also in building powerful data systems that target the right services to the right students in the right schools at the right time. The good news is that we know much more about how to do that than ever before" (Peltzman & Jerald, 2006, p. 8).

The Bill & Melinda Gates Foundation has issued a series of briefs intended to support district efforts to tackle the dropout problem. In one of them (2010), school leaders are encouraged to focus on answering the following "three big questions":

- Which indicators best predict who will not graduate?
- Who is on track, at each grade level, to graduate?
- Who is at risk, off track, and likely to fail? Knowing these students by name and knowing where they go to school will be key to intervening on their behalf.

The brief suggests that school leaders

> answer the first question by analyzing recent history to learn which indicators are the strongest predictors of future dropouts. Then use these indicators to segment current students into groups and target interventions more effectively. (Bill & Melinda Gates Foundation, 2010, p. 5)

Using Data About Students Off-Track for Graduation: Some Guiding Questions

- What are the most prevalent indicators or symptoms among the students who are off-track?
- Can you group off-track students by indicator (e.g., students who are off track because of attendance, course performance, all indicators, etc.)?
- Were current off-track students also off-track at the end of their previous grade (or as they entered from the feeder schools)?
- What are the demographics of students identified as "off-track" (e.g., NCLB subgroups or other characteristics) for graduation?
- What other data are important to include for the discussion? For example:
  - In which classes or types of classes are groups of off-track students enrolled (e.g., remedial reading or mathematics courses)? Is it possible to group students by common needs (e.g., improving literacy) as opposed to by common indicators (e.g., failing English/language arts)?
  - Are there any patterns in reasons for absence amongst students who are off-track because of attendance flags?
  - Are there any notable out-of-school characteristics that off-track students share or exhibit (e.g., single parent homes, low socioeconomic status, pregnancy or teenage parent, etc.)?
  - Are there common behavior characteristics amongst off-track students?
  - Are there any underlying school climate issues that may be causing students to disengage from school?
  - What conjectures regarding reasons for students' off-track status can you make based on your observations?

Source: National High School Center, 2009, p. 8.

Research has found that risk factors or indicators tend to fall into two major categories—low academic performance (e.g., low grades or test scores, falling behind in required course credits, and retention in grade) and educational engagement (e.g., high rates of truancy or absenteeism, disciplinary problems, and low participation in extracurricular activities; Jerald, 2006). Obviously, many students may exhibit combinations of these risk factors since, for example, missing many days of school will lead to low grades, with the student then feeling even less motivated to attend regularly. In addition, "there might not be one single 'leading indicator'.... In other words, for many dropouts, 'one thing can lead to another.' But it is not always the *same* thing" (Jerald, 2006, p. 16). Jerald also stresses that school-related factors—such as low grades or absenteeism—associated with high drop-out rates should be given special attention by educators:

> because they are *practical* and because they are *predictive*.... As such, they can be helpful in determining the kinds of interventions that students might need and that education systems can provide. (2006, p. 5)

However, "identifying students at risk of dropping out by using an early warning system is only the first step in addressing the drop-out challenge" (Heppen & Therriault, 2008, p. 7). In a comprehensive approach to addressing the drop-out problem, schools should:

- Provide intervention strategies for students who are identified as most at risk, with strategies tailored to meet the needs of the individual student (e.g., help with a particular course needed for graduation vs. more general supports). "Most promising are efforts that combine more personalized education with enhanced academic supports and college and career ready curricula" (Balfanz et al., 2009, p. 15).

- Monitor at-risk students to gauge whether the impact of the interventions will likely be enough to help them through to graduation. Change or intensify the supports if necessary.
- Monitor students who—while not thought to be at a critical level of risk—might still need extra help. These students could be served through less-intensive supports such as special monitoring from their teachers.
- Identify and address schoolwide areas of concern that may be negatively affecting students in ways that make it more likely they will drop out—for example, what Roderick (1993) called the "critical junctures" (p. 145) of the transitions from elementary to middle school and middle to high school or suspension policies that contribute to students' academic problems.

Finally, districts must recognize that dropouts are not simply a high school problem. For many dropouts, the potential for dropping out could have been identified—and addressed—as early as elementary school. Elementary and middle schools must be part of the district strategy to address the dropout problem, and conversations among educators at the different school levels are critical to finding ways to better support students.

"Most dropouts:

- Are identifiable years before they dropout.
- Struggle in or disengage from school for three to four or more years before they dropout.
- Are preventable.
- Ultimately want to graduate from high school." (Balfanz, 2008)

Provide Multiple Graduation Options

Obviously, schools and districts should be evaluating their programs on a continuing basis to ensure that they graduate students who are career and college ready. However, there is an additional element that should be addressed when looking at the issue of dropout prevention or of encouraging dropouts to reengage with school. This approach has even been given a name—Multiple Pathways to Graduation. Typically, the programs address key elements such as scheduling issues (for example, "twilight" programs that meet in the evening), students' need for special supports in areas such as reading skills, and a curriculum that addresses preparation for work or postsecondary education. Jobs for the Future (JFF; 2009) has developed the following questions schools or districts can use in planning interventions to help what they describe as "off-track students" who are either over-age and likely to drop out or who have already dropped out:

- What data, if any, do you have that segment the off-track population based on academic profile at the district and/or school-programming level? What do they tell you about the populations that need recuperative schools/programs?
- For which of these population(s) of youth does your community have schools or programs that are showing evidence of effectiveness? Are these schools or programs serving populations of students based on their academic profiles or on other factors? If other factors, which ones?
- For which populations do you need additional or more effective models?
- What immediate steps might you take to improve the models already in place or create new options to close the gap for those not well served?

> Go to the Web site of the Youth Transitions Funders Group (http://www.ytfg.org) to download *Closing the Graduation Gap: A Superintendent's Guide for Planning Multiple Pathways to Graduation* as well as other resources on Multiple Pathways to Graduation.
>
> Download the report directly from: http://www.ytfg.org/documents/ClosingtheGraduationGapFinal13October2008.pdf

Based on its work in several school districts, JFF has also developed brief descriptions of educational options designed for populations with specific characteristics. A few of these are included on the next page:

- Over-age/off-track students age 16 or older, with enough credits/skill to graduate in 3 years—Academically rigorous diploma-granting high schools with personalized learning environments, rigorous academic standards, student-centered pedagogy, acceleration strategies for academic catch-up, wraparound support to meet instructional/developmental goals, and clear pathways to college.
- Over-age/off-track students age 17 or older, with enough skills/credits to graduate in 1 year—Flexible programming to allow students to make up credits quickly while gaining skills for the transition to postsecondary learning, interdisciplinary curricula that meet multiple credit requirements and/or self-paced academic work in needed credit areas, wraparound supports to meet instructional/developmental goals, and focus on connections to college.
- Over-age/off-track students age 17 or older, with few credits/low skills, and an eighth-grade reading level—GED-granting programs with clear pathways/interim benchmarks through community college featuring intensive literacy across the curriculum, student-centered pedagogy, clear systems for ongoing assessment, pathways to postsecondary training/learning, and in-depth, sector-specific career exploration (2009, p. 62).

The Institute of Education Sciences (IES) of the U.S. Department of Education convened a panel of researchers to review research relevant to dropout prevention. The panel made six recommendations:

- Utilize data systems that support a realistic diagnosis of the number of students who drop out and help identify individual students at high risk of dropping out (diagnostic).
- Assign adult advocates to students at risk of dropping out (targeted intervention).
- Provide academic support and enrichment to improve academic performance (targeted intervention).
- Implement programs to improve students' classroom behavior and social skills (targeted intervention).
- Personalize the learning environment and instructional process (schoolwide intervention).
- Provide rigorous and relevant instruction to better engage students in learning and provide the skills needed to graduate and to serve them after they leave school (schoolwide intervention; Dynarski et al., 2008).

Include the Broader Community in Efforts to Address the Dropout Problem

Including community groups as partners has been a key element in the dropout prevention efforts of many school districts. The challenge for districts and schools is to encourage groups such as the Chamber of Commerce or local religious organizations to join the conversation about what they can do to emphasize the message to young people and their families that high school graduation is important and, also, to support these students through internships, the availability of safe places for studying after school, and a host of other possibilities.

On a national level, a report issued by the Everyone Graduates Center at Johns Hopkins University identified some heartening trends related to this need.

> A much broader spectrum of the nation is getting involved in [ensuring] that all students graduate from high school. The dropout crisis is no longer seen as simply a school problem.... Growing numbers of social change organizations, including the United Way, City Year, Communities In Schools and the Boys and Girls clubs, have made the nation's graduation rate one of their core missions. The America's Promise Alliance has launched an ambitious national effort to galvanize community efforts to end the dropout crisis by sponsoring dropout prevention summits in all 50 states and 55 cities. The Department of Labor has launched several initiatives aimed at increasing graduation rates in medium and large cities and public health professionals have recognized dropout prevention as a key to community well-being. (Balfanz & West, 2009, p. 14)

References

Alliance for Excellent Education. (2008). *From no child left behind to every child a graduate.* Washington, DC: Author. Retrieved from http://www.all4ed.org/files/ECAG.pdf

Alliance for Excellent Education. (2010). Prioritizing the nation's lowest-performing high schools: The need for targeted federal policy (Issue Brief). Washington, DC: Author. Retrieved from http://www.all4ed.org/files/PrioritizingLowestPerformingSchools.pdf

Balfanz, R. (2008, January 20). *Three steps to building an early warning and intervention system for potential dropouts.* Presentation. Retrieved from http://www.every1graduates.org/PDFs/Three_Steps.pdf

Balfanz, R., & Legters, N. (2004). *Locating the dropout crisis.* Baltimore: Johns Hopkins University Center for Social Organization of Schools. Retrieved from http://www.csos.jhu.edu/crespar/techReports/Report70.pdf

Balfanz, R., & West, T. C. (2009). *Raising graduation rates—A series of data briefs: Progress toward increasing the national and state graduation rates*. Baltimore: Everyone Graduates. Retrieved from http://www.every1graduates.org/PDFs/StateProgressReport.pdf

Balfanz, R., Fox, J. H., Bridgeland, J. M., & McNaught, M. (2009). *Grad nation: A guidebook to help communities tackle the dropout crisis*. Washington, DC: America's Promise Alliance. Retrieved from http://www.americaspromise.org/Our-Work/Dropout-Prevention/Grad-Nation-Guidebook.aspx

Bill & Melinda Gates Foundation. (2010). *This school works for me: Creating choices to boost achievement (An implementation guide for school district administrators)*. Seattle, WA: Author. Retrieved from http://www.gatesfoundation.org/united-states/Documents/school-works-for-me-implementation-guide.pdf

Bridgeland, J. M., DiIulio, J. J., & Morison, K. B. (2006). *The silent epidemic: Perspectives of high school dropouts*. Retrieved from http://www.civicenterprises.net/pdfs/thesilentepidemic3-06.pdf

Dynarski, M., Clarke, L., Cobb, B., Finn, J., Rumberger, R., & Smink, J. (2008). *Dropout prevention: A practice guide* (NCEE 2008–4025). Washington, DC: National Center for Education Evaluation and Regional Assistance, Institute of Education Sciences, U.S. Department of Education. Retrieved from http://ies.ed.gov/ncee/wwc

Heppen, J. B., & Therriault, S. B. (2008). Developing early warning systems to identify potential high school dropouts. Washington, DC: National High School Center. Retrieved from http://www.betterhighschools.org/docs/IssueBrief_EarlyWarningSystemsGuide_081408.pdf

Jerald, C. D. (2006). *Identifying potential dropouts: Key lessons for building an early warning data system*. Washington, DC: Achieve, Inc., American Diploma Project Network. Retrieved from http://www.achieve.org/files/FINAL-dropouts_0.pdf

Jobs for the Future. (2009). *Bringing off-track youth into the center of high school reform: Lessons and tools from leading communities*. Boston, MA: Author. Retrieved from http://www.jff.org/sites/default/files/strategic_toolkit072209.pdf

MetisNet. (2008). *Closing the graduation gap: A superintendent's guide for planning multiple pathways to graduation*. Chicago: Youth Transitions Funders Group. Retrieved from http://www.ytfg.org/documents/ClosingtheGraduationGapFinal13October2008.pdf

National High School Center. (2009). *A practitioner's guide to analyzing Virginia's Early Warning System data* (Draft). Washington, DC: Author.

Peltzman, A. & Jerald, C. (2006, December). High standards and high graduation rates: Using data-driven dropout preventions strategies will be key to ensuring that all students learn more and stay in school. *State Education Standard*, 7-13.

Roderick, M. (1993). *The path to dropping out: Evidence for intervention.* Westport, CT: Auburn House.

Chapter 3:
The Achievement Gap

The Talk

Schools aren't making any progress on closing the achievement gap.

The Truth

Yes, we do have schools in which too little progress is being made to close the gap. But there are also schools that have made substantial gains. And we have some data that indicate gaps are narrowing.

> "In 1996, nearly three of every four African-American fourth-graders could not perform at a basic level in mathematics. By 2007, that was down to 30 percent. This is a real testament to the hard work of educators and students across the country. But we cannot for a minute rest on this success." (The Education Trust, 2009)

Let's turn first to national data. The National Center for Education Statistics (NCES) develops a "report card" for the nation using data from the National Assessment of Educational Progress (NAEP) assessments, and a 2009 report focused specifically on the Black-White achievement gap. Results indicated some narrowing of the gap, although a substantial gap still exists:

> In 2007, mathematics scores for both Black and White public school students in grades 4 and 8 nationwide, as measured by the main NAEP assessments of the National Assessment of Educational Progress (NAEP), were higher than in any previous assessment, going back to 1990. This was also true for Black and White fourth-graders on the NAEP 2007 Reading Assessment. For grade 8, reading scores for both Black and White students were higher in 2007 than in the first reading assessment year, 1992, as well as the most recent previous assessment year, 2005.
>
> White students, however, had higher scores than Black students, on average, on all assessments. While the nationwide gaps in 2007 were narrower than in previous assessments at both grades 4 and 8 in mathematics and at grade 4 in reading, White students had average scores at least 26 points higher than Black students in each subject, on a 0-500 scale. (Vanneman, Hamilton, Baldwin Anderson, & Rahman, 2009, p. iii)

Another source of information is the Center for Education Policy (CEP). This organization periodically conducts a trend analysis of student achievement data from state testing systems. A 2009 analysis looked specifically at both overall trends in achievement and also at the achievement gap. The Center found some heartening trends:

- **All subgroups showed more gains than declines in grade 4 at all three achievement levels—basic-and-above, proficient-and-above, and advanced.** Trends varied, however, by subject and subgroup. Subgroup results were more positive in math than in reading at all achievement levels. Four-fifths or more of the states with adequate data made gains in math for nearly all subgroups at both the proficient and advanced levels. Progress in math was particularly noteworthy for Latino students scoring at or above the proficient level, where 95% of the states with data improved, and for African Americans scoring at the advanced level, where 91% of the states with data made gains. In reading, subgroup gains were more common at the proficient level than at the basic or advanced level.

- **As measured by percentages of students scoring proficient, gaps between subgroups have narrowed in most states at the elementary, middle, and high school levels, although gaps have widened in a notable minority of cases.** In both reading and math, gaps in percentages proficient narrowed in 74% of instances the CEP studied and widened in 23% of instances. For example, the African American-White gap in 4th-grade reading narrowed in 28 of the 36 states with adequate data, widened in 7 states, and showed no change in 1 state. Across subgroups and states, there was more progress in closing gaps at the elementary and middle school levels than at the high school level. Even with this progress, however, the gaps between subgroups often remained large—upwards of 20 percentage points in many cases.

- **Most often gaps narrowed because the achievement of lower-performing subgroups went up rather than because the achievement of higher-performing subgroups went down.** When gaps narrowed, it was usually because both of the subgroups being compared made gains, but the target group (such as Latino students) improved at a greater rate than the comparison group (such as White students). When gaps widened, it was most often because both subgroups made gains but the comparison group improved at a greater rate than the target group.

- **Although average (mean) scores indicate that gaps have narrowed more often than they have widened, mean scores give a less rosy picture of progress in closing achievement gaps than percentages proficient.** In the states with both mean score and percentage proficient data, gaps narrowed 59% of the time using mean scores, compared with 71% of the time using percentages proficient. Mean score gaps also widened more often than percentage proficient gaps—37% of the time for mean scores versus 24% of the time for percentages proficient. Even so, mean scores for subgroups have risen in most cases, and gaps in mean scores have narrowed in the majority of instances (Chudowsky, Chudowsky, & Kober, 2009, pp. 1-2).

The report's authors go on to summarize the "good news" from their study:

> Overall, states have made progress in closing achievement gaps, as measured by the percentage of students in various subgroups reaching the proficient level on state tests. In 74% of all cases, gaps in percentages proficient narrowed. In other words, the improvements made by target subgroups were larger than the gains shown by comparison subgroups. Also, many people tend to assume the worst when they hear that achievement gaps are widening, as was the case in 23% of cases. It is important to remember that even in most of these instances, subgroup achievement still improved, although not at the same rate as for

> white and non-low-income students. Therefore, partly as a result of this pattern of overall improvement, progress on achievement gaps is slow and uneven. Still, it is encouraging to see progress in grade 4 among all subgroups across all three achievement levels—basic, proficient, and advanced—although there is some variation among subgroups. (Chudowsky, Chudowsky, & Kober, 2009, p. 22)

> "Let's start by stating the obvious: With or without No Child Left Behind, closing the disparities in achievement for students of color, low-income students and English language learners is the right thing to do." (Ray-Taylor, 2005)

The Crucial Conversations

Complex is a word that quickly comes to mind when thinking about achievement gaps—and of ways to tackle them. Downey and her fellow authors talk about this:

> The first important step to take in confronting the achievement gap problem is to abandon the idea that one single thing, or even a few things in combination, will crack this apparently baffling educational conundrum. And the very first factor to confront is that there is no single "achievement gap" but many kinds of gaps. (Downey, Steffy, Poston, & English, 2009, p. 1)

The causes for the achievement gap are also complex. Typically, they are discussed as falling into two main categories: 1) factors related to students' socioeconomic status, cultural environment, and family background; and 2) factors related to students' schools.

Socio-Cultural Causes. One of the main factors associated with low student achievement is poverty. Students living in persistent poverty are more likely than other students to suffer from many conditions that impede their learning, for example:

- poor health care (including inadequate prenatal care for their mothers);
- frequent changes in residence, requiring transferring to new schools repeatedly; and,
- lack of books and other educational resources in the home.

Cultural attitudes and racism also play a part in the achievement gap. Research suggests that some minority students feel that the majority culture sees them as less capable and expects little of them. These students may not try in school, since they believe they won't succeed anyway.

School-Related Causes. Unfortunately, students who start out with disadvantages often encounter school conditions that only add to the problem. Research has repeatedly found they are more likely to attend schools with inadequate funding staffed with teachers who are not as qualified to teach their subjects as teachers in other schools. In addition, especially in schools with high concentrations of poor and minority students, some teachers may have low expectations of these students, adding to the problem of already low expectations these students may have for their own futures.

Thus, the crucial conversations highlighted below represent only a few of the topics that could be addressed by thoughtful, comprehensive efforts to talk about reducing achievement gaps. But they do represent a place to start:

- Broaden the review of data.
- Expand responsibilities for student support past the schoolhouse doors.
- Review "what works" in other schools.
- Address hard issues such as race and low expectations.

Broaden the Review of Data

Researchers from The Education Trust suggest that looking at gaps means more than simply looking at the current size of gaps between groups. In their view, districts and schools should also ask:

- Have all groups of students gained over time?
- Have absolute gaps in mean performance between groups decreased over time?
- How does each group of students currently perform compared with their counterparts in other jurisdictions? (Rowan, Hall, & Haycock, 2010)

This review of data should be followed by discussions about the possible implications of the data and ways in which schools might apply the "messages" to gap-reduction efforts. For example, if the pattern of gaps among schools with previously similar results has shifted, districts and their schools should look to schools that have been more successful for reasons—and for approaches—that might be incorporated in the programs of the less successful schools.

In addition, Ferguson (2007) suggests a broader range of issues should be part of gap conversations that are informed by data. These include looking at nonschool factors that may impact students—for example, student mobility. Even though this is an outside-school factor, schools and districts may be able to help their highly mobile students who change schools as well as their homes by ensuring that there are common standards, curricula, and pacing calendars across schools. Student absenteeism significantly higher for students on the "wrong" side of a gap also deserves attention by schools, perhaps through increased communication with families.

Other factors identified by Ferguson are even more within the control of schools and so represent especially important opportunities for data-informed conversations. For example, an analysis of data may identify disproportionate numbers of students from specific racial-ethnic groups underrepresented in gifted programs or AP classes or overrepresented in special education programs or in disciplinary actions. While none of these conditions can be addressed by easy fixes, they all represent circumstances that can affect student achievement results as well as the broader issue of equitable treatment for all students.

"It is a poor policy indeed that erects huge barriers to the success of millions of students, cherry-picks and praises a few schools that appear to clear those barriers, and then blames the other schools for their failure to do the same. Yet the nation, through NCLB and the writings of people like those just cited, has effectively adopted this outcomes-oriented, input-ignoring philosophy. Policy makers pay great attention to 'the achievement gap' that exists between poor and more-advantaged students and, via NCLB, now even require that schools eliminate the gap completely by 2014. This approach is perfectly sensible if divorced from the actual schooling context. But in the real world outputs have relationships to inputs that cannot be ignored." (Berliner, 2009, pp. 5-6)

Expand Responsibilities for Student Support Past the Schoolhouse Doors

Educators know that the experiences—both past and present—that students bring to school can have a dramatic impact on students' ability to succeed in school. Quite simply, "children whose basic needs are not met cannot come to school ready to learn" (Gándara, 2010, p. 5). However, if educators point to nonschool problems as barriers to learning, it is sometimes seen as simply offering excuses for the school's lack of success with educating all students. Rothstein talks about this:

> Some school reformers fear that any mention of socioeconomic influences on learning will be used as "excuses" for poor teaching. But we can't avoid excuses by promoting simplistic myths about educational processes. Instead, those making excuses for poor performance should be challenged, corrected, or if necessary, removed.
>
> The alternative—pretending that more effective schools can close achievement gaps on their own—promises the impossible, setting schools and teachers up for failure. Why shouldn't the public conclude that schools are incompetent if educators cannot achieve what some foolishly promise?
>
> I am often accused of letting schools "off the hook" by making this argument. Not at all—both schools and social policy need improvement. But claims that schools alone can close achievement gaps let politicians and business leaders "off the hook." We let them claim one day that it's too expensive to provide health insurance to all children, and on the next pose as advocates for minorities by demanding that schools close the gap. (2007)

> "Schools alone cannot redress the achievement gap. Responsibility for education extends beyond the schools, necessitating a comprehensive set of strategies that actively invite families, communities, and businesses onto the school campus. Schools must actively and willingly invite new partners into the process of education." (Poliakoff, 2006)

The Schott Foundation for Public Education focuses much of its efforts on improving educational outcomes for African American boys, a subgroup disproportionately affected by the gap problem. While the foundation recognizes the impact schools can have, it also takes a broader perspective and highlights the need to engage the broader community:

> Many more people must get involved in multiple efforts. This certainly includes individuals and families, and also includes local institutions such as faith-based institutions, small businesses and larger corporations, local colleges and universities, and both private and public foundations. (Sen, 2006, p. 4)

In talking about achievement problems of low-income students, Varlas also talks about the need for crucial conversations about closing achievement gaps to address issues beyond the schoolhouse door:

> If community characteristics such as poverty are strongly associated with student achievement, then efforts to improve student performance must focus on the community as a whole, not just on the school. (2008, para. 3)

Full-service community schools in which community agencies partner with schools to provide critically important health and social services for students and their families at the school site could be one key element in these crucial conversations. Arne Duncan, U.S. Secretary of Education, characterizes them as "a triumph of common sense" (Blank, Berg, & Melaville, 2006, p. 16). Clarke talks about the approach:

> A common misconception is that schools are going to be asked to do even more. However, while schools are natural community hubs, it is not feasible for a school to start offering and funding an array of services. The key to integrated services, therefore, is partnership. Partnerships are fundamental to a community school. Generally speaking, communities have multiple organizations and agencies working towards the same end—positive youth outcomes, healthy families, and strong communities. Yet, these services are scattered in various locations and work in solitude. The idea is to identify and bring together disparate providers under one roof in partnership with the school so that each entity can help one another achieve their goals. (Clarke, 2009, p. 2)

Obviously, bringing together the school, community agencies, and other organizations will take focused collaborative efforts. Clarke stresses that planning will need to address "working out the kinks" (2009, p. 8) since the collaboration will ask "practitioners from different professions with different training, different codes of ethics, and different languages to share resources, people, and space in order to accomplish common goals" (2009, p. 8). While full-service community schools represent only one way to address the needs students bring with them to school, it is a start.

Review "What Works" in Other Schools

While much of the work necessary to reduce the achievement gap is outside the control of schools, there are some things that schools can do—and are doing—to raise achievement for all students. School efforts should be guided by research that suggests that factors such as the following can help narrow the achievement gap:

- Cultural congruence in instruction. When there is a good match between the student's and teacher's respective knowledge bases—as there usually is between White, middle-class students and their teachers—then achievement tends to be high. If teachers can find ways to structure their teaching so they tap into their minority students' stores of knowledge, student achievement may improve dramatically.
- Teaching strategies that promote meaningful participation. These include cooperative learning activities, as well as instructional approaches that are flexible enough to appeal to individual students' interests and abilities.
- Approaches that address the needs of struggling students before they are so far behind that they can never catch up.

Since 2004, the Kentucky Department of Education has engaged in a project that identifies closing-the-gap schools and then summarizes "common themes" from the practices of these schools. Their 2008-2009 study found that the schools studied all "had an intentional plan for closing their achievement gaps that could be clearly articulated" (2009, p. 7). In addition, four categories of themes—along with strategies—were presented:

Student Achievement. The schools closing their achievement gaps:

- Aligned curriculum to Kentucky Program of Studies and Core Content (common assessments, short- & long-term student and school goals);
- Defined what students needed to know and be able to do (curriculum maps/pacing guides);
- Provided a master schedule with full access to the core content curriculum for all students, intentionally designed the schedule to match teacher strengths with student need, intentionally planned for effective collaboration;
- Organized teachers to regularly collaborate on analyzing student work, put protocols in place to help organize planning time and analyze student work, developed common planning into master schedule for all teachers (early release days, grade/team/faculty meetings);
- Collected, analyzed, and used multiple survey data for planning (comprehensive school improvement plan, Title 1 schoolwide plan, parent involvement activities); and,
- Regularly analyzed and evaluated student achievement data to plan instruction.

School Community (certified/classified staff, councils, students, families, community members). The schools closing their achievement gaps:

- Intentionally allocated resources and provided a framework with the primary focus on removing barriers (extended school services);
- Maximized opportunities for students through individual schedules for all to have access to teachers' instructional strengths (flexible scheduling and enrichment classes); and,
- Provided outlets for teachers to share innovative ideas.

Culture (school culture and climate, culturally responsive teaching & instruction). The schools closing their achievement gaps:

- Encouraged teachers to acknowledge their responsibility in student success and failure (a staff with a "whatever it takes" and "by any means necessary" attitude);
- Praised staff members who regularly interact with students (i.e., formal/informal communication);
- Developed teachers who regularly contact families to discuss academic and behavior success, as well as deficiencies;
- Provided professional development that addressed professional practice to challenge, engage, and motivate students for higher learning; and,
- Developed teachers' schedules to provide opportunities to share and discuss student progress (professional learning communities and common planning).

Celebrations (formal and informal recognition of students). The schools closing their achievement gaps:

- Hosted regular, equitable, cost effective, formal and informal celebrations to recognize students for academics, behavior and effort; and,
- Shared academic achievement with the family and community stakeholders (family nights, local newspaper, board meetings, and business marquees). (Excerpted from Kentucky Department of Education, 2009, pp. 6-7.)

As another example of research that can inform school practice, Jesse, Davis, and Pokorny studied a sample of middle schools in which Latino students from low-income families made substantial gains in achievement. Characteristics of the schools most consistent with previous research on effective schools included "the presence of strong schoolwide leadership that connected with the community, teacher expertise and expectations, and frequent home-school communications" (2004, pp. 31-32).

While many of these "strategies" need to receive attention at the school level, others should be addressed by school district policies and practices. For example, if schools in the district that are most likely to serve low-performing students are also found to have teaching staff that are, in general, less experienced or less effective, explicit efforts should be made to shift highly effective teachers to these schools.

Address Hard Issues Such as Race and Low Expectations

Relationships between teachers and students make a difference. The National Study Group for the Affirmative Development of Academic Ability studied "the continued academic underperformance of students of color" (2004, p. 1) and identified building trust and confidence of minority students in their teachers and schools as important to their engagement in education.

Research conducted by Ronald Ferguson, a researcher long involved with studying the achievement gap, may provide one reason why this trust is important to student learning. Ferguson surveyed middle and high school students in school districts participating in the Minority Student Achievement Network. Black students were much more likely than White students to say that teacher encouragement—as contrasted with teacher demand—was the reason they "worked hard." Students defined teacher encouragement as including three key elements:

- The teacher lets you know he or she really believes you can do it.
- The teacher lets you know that he or she is there for you. You may not have a problem but if you do, the teacher is there to help.
- The teacher lets you know that your success really matters to him or her. The teacher has an emotional stake in your success. (Ferguson, 2004, p. 10)

> "When the Task Force talked with the boys, teens, and young men for whom we wrote this report, they told us that—most of all—they want teachers who care for them, who believe in them, who expect as much from them as anyone else, and who will give them as much.... They want rigor and discipline tempered with compassion and love. They want their school staffed with people who don't think authority and empathy are mutually exclusive or that equity is impossible. They want teachers and administrators who aren't afraid of them but aren't afraid to care about them either. The young men we talked to weren't angry. They were hurting. And they didn't feel forgotten as much as they felt forsaken." (Task Force on the Education of Maryland's African-American Males, 2006, p. 3)

In a study of the impact of school reform on students, students stressed the importance of teacher caring and teacher-student relationships. In their view, they worked harder for teachers who cared about them. At the same time, it was important to the students that their teachers "pushed" them to succeed and showed by their actions that they believed the students could achieve. Unfortunately, not all teachers fuse caring and high expectations. Wasley, Hampel, and Clark (1997) found many of the teachers they observed exhibited caring—but not high expectations. Other research supports both the importance of high expectations and the variety of subtle ways in which a message of less than high expectations can be communicated by teachers—for example, by asking easier questions of students they consider to be at risk.

The bottom line is that teachers and other staff members need to become more conscious of their own attitudes and behaviors, so that they don't unintentionally communicate low expectations. This may require hard conversations. Alson talks about important information for these conversations that can be garnered by asking students for feedback about how they view their interactions with school:

> Student struggles and successes told in their own voices offer great insights into their attitudes toward and their experiences with school. They also yield strong suggestions as to how to reinforce what works well and how to remove barriers that block success. (Alson, 2003, p. 5)

References

Alson, A. (2003, Fall). The academic achievement gap: The suburban challenge. *CSR Connection*, 1-10.

Berliner, D. C. (2009). *Poverty and potential: Out-of-school factors and school success.* Boulder and Tempe, CO: Education and the Public Interest Center & Education Policy Research Unit. Retrieved from http://epicpolicy.org/publication/poverty-and-potential

Blank, M. J., Berg, A. C., & Melaville, A. (2006). *Growing community schools: The role of cross-boundary leadership.* Washington, DC: Coalition for Community Schools, Institute for Educational Leadership.

Chudowsky, N., Chudowsky, V., & Kober, N. (2009). *State test score trends through 2007-08: Are achievement gaps closing and is achievement rising for all?* Washington, DC: Center on Education Policy. Retrieved from http://www.cep-dc.org/index.cfm?fuseaction=document_ext.showDocumentByID&nodeID=1&DocumentID=292

Clarke, S. (2009). *ERS informed educator: Full-service community schools: Bringing together the services your students need.* Alexandria, VA: Educational Research Service.

Downey, C. J., Steffy, B. E., Poston, W. K., & English, F. W. (2009). *50 ways to close the achievement gap* (3rd ed.). Thousand Oaks, CA: Corwin Press.

The Education Trust. (2009). Closing the gaps. Retrieved from http://www.edtrust.org/issues/pre-k-12/closing-the-gaps

Ferguson, R. (2004, July 3). *Professional community and closing the achievement gap.* Presentation at Advocating for What's Right: A One-Day NEA Symposium on Critical Issues for Educators.

Ferguson, R. F. (2007). *Toward excellence with equity: An emerging vision for closing the achievement gap.* Cambridge, MA: Harvard University Press.

Gándara, P. (2010). *The Latino education crisis: Rescuing the American dream.* San Francisco, CA: WestEd. Retrieved from http://www.wested.org/online_pubs/pp-10-02.pdf

Jesse, D., Davis, A., & Pokorny, N. (2004). High-achieving middle schools for Latino students in poverty. *Journal of Education for Students Placed at Risk, 90*(1), 23-45.

Kentucky Department of Education. (2009). *Achievement gap data review explanation.* Retrieved from http://www.education.ky.gov/KDE/Instructional+Resources/Closing+the+Gap/Achievement+Gap+Data.htm

National Center for Education Statistics. (2009). *Achievement gaps: How Black and White students in public schools perform on the National Assessment of Educational Progress (highlights).* Retrieved from http://nces.ed.gov/nationsreportcard/pdf/studies/2009495.pdf

The National Study Group for the Affirmative Development of Academic Ability. (2004). *All students reaching the top: Strategies for closing academic achievement gaps.* Naperville, IL: Learning Point Associates.

Poliakoff, A. R. (2006, January). *ASCD Infobrief: Closing the gap: An overview.* Retrieved from http://www.ascd.org/publications/newsletters/infobrief/jan06/num44/toc.aspx

Ray-Taylor, R. (2005, January). Lessons learned about the achievement gap. *The School Administrator.* Retrieved from http://www.aasa.org/SchoolAdministratorArticle.aspx?id=8832&terms=Ray-taylor

Rothstein, R. (2007, November 28). What's causing the gap? *Los Angeles Times.* Retrieved from http://www.latimes.com/news/opinion/la-op-dustup28nov28,0,3320609.story

Rowan, A. H., Hall, D., & Haycock, K. (2010). *Gauging the gaps: A deeper look at student achievement.* Retrieved from http://www.edtrust.org/sites/edtrust.org/files/publications/files/NAEP%20Gap_0.pdf

Sen, R. (2006). *A positive future for Black boys: Building the movement.* Cambridge, MA: Schott Foundation for Public Education. Retrieved from http://www.schottfoundation.org/publications/Schott_Positive%20Future_7.pdf

Task Force on the Education of Maryland's African-American Males. (2006). *Task Force on the Education of Maryland's African-American Males.* Annapolis, MD: Maryland K–16 Leadership Council. Retrieved from http://www.eric.ed.gov/ERICDocs/data/ericdocs2sql/content_storage_01/0000019b/80/28/0e/00.pdf

Vanneman, A., Hamilton, L., Baldwin Anderson, J., & Rahman, T. (2009). *Achievement gaps: How Black and White students in public schools perform in mathematics and reading on the National Assessment of Educational Progress, (NCES 2009-455).* Washington, DC: National Center for Education Statistics, Institute of Education Sciences, U.S. Department of Education. Retrieved from http://nces.ed.gov/nationsreportcard/pdf/studies/2009455.pdf

Varlas, L. (2008, Summer). *ASCD InfoBrief: Full-service community schools.* Retrieved from http://www.ascd.org/publications/newsletters/infobrief/summer08/num54/full/Full-Service_Community_Schools.aspx

Wasley, P. A., Hampel, R. L., & Clark, R. W. (1997). *Kids and school reform.* San Francisco: Jossey-Bass.

Chapter 4:
Turning Around Low-Performing Schools

The Talk

Some schools are so bad you have to clear out the staff and start over!

The Truth

While there are undoubtedly some schools so "broken" that starting over seems the only remedy, these represent a small percentage of schools across our country. The flip side of the coin is the thousands of schools that are doing their jobs—including many that have improved substantially and rapidly in the last few years.

Let's look at the most daunting challenges. The Adequate Yearly Progress (AYP) provision of the No Child Left Behind Act (NCLB)—along with some state accountability systems that preceded NCLB—had already focused attention on low-performing schools. However, the U.S. Department of Education has recently raised the stakes—and the requirements placed on states, districts, and schools—even higher. The awarding of School Improvement Grants for school districts through the states has now been linked to a framework that channels these funds to districts with persistently low-achieving schools that "demonstrate the greatest need for the funds *and the strongest commitment to use those funds to raise substantially the achievement of the students attending those schools*" (emphasis added). A district that applies for funding must identify the schools it intends to serve and also which of four Department of Education-specified "school intervention models intended to improve the management and effectiveness of these schools" that it will implement (U.S. Department of Education, 2009, p. 65,617). Incremental, slow-paced change is not an option for these schools.

Thus, districts with schools classified as persistently low-achieving will have to struggle with decisions about what approach to take and, certainly just as important, how to implement it effectively. Dedicated, hard-working educators working in these schools, as well as students and their families, will be affected in fundamental ways. Most worrisome, there is no guarantee that the approach taken in any one school will guarantee success. So thoughtful discussions about how to approach these changes will be critical.

But let's not forget schools that are already producing high levels of student achievement, and especially, schools that have already turned themselves around. This story is also part of the "truth" about public education although it may not receive sufficient attention. These schools' successes and the roads they have taken to achieve them should also be addressed in crucial conversations about a community's educational system.

> "I know that change is possible. I know we have the talent and ideas to succeed. The only question is whether we have the courage to do what's right for kids. We've seen what happens when caution trumps courage. Nothing changes and kids lose. But we've also seen the opposite—where bold leaders have fought the status quo. We've seen traditional public schools where creative and dedicated educators built strong teams, boosted parental involvement, and raised student achievement." (Duncan, 2009, p. 5)

Crucial Conversations

On the national scene—and in too many communities—rhetoric about a failing system of public schools diverts attention from crucial conversations that could help to strengthen schools and ensure that all children receive a high-quality education. Some of these conversations should be held in schools, some at the district level or between district and school staff, and others should engage parents and other community members in dialogue with educators. But the goal of all these conversations needs to shift away from "bashing" public education and toward a focus on identifying ways to ensure that all schools are high performing. Topics such as the following support that goal:

- Painting a true picture of public schools—and student achievement—in our communities.
- Recognizing that districts must be part of the solution.
- Focusing on principal leadership.
- Making hard decisions about persistently low-performing schools.

Painting a True Picture of Public Schools—and Student Achievement—in Our Communities

Schools and districts across the country have their own good news stories about efforts to either keep student achievement high or raise it. Within each community, educators should spread the good news and ensure that these success stories are part of the conversation. But those outside education too often don't hear about successes happening elsewhere, and it's important that messages about these be communicated as well.

For example, a report recently issued by the Brown Center on Education Policy announced:

> Big city schools have made significant gains. While all school districts have notched achievement gains, the big city districts made even larger gains than other districts. They are closing the gap with suburban and rural districts, slowly, to be sure, but they are clearly making progress. (Loveless, 2009, p. 5)

This growth in achievement has also been reported by the Council of Great City Schools. In 50 urban districts, large gains were made in mathematics and smaller—but still statistically significant—gains were made in reading (Snipe, Horwitz, Soga, & Casserly, 2008).

For another good news story, Whitehurst points to "dramatically rising mathematics performance on the National Assessment of Education Progress" as an indication that U.S. public schools can implement changes that have positive impacts on student learning:

> Average performance at fourth grade rose 14 points between 2000 and 2007, representing well over a year's worth of schooling. Increases were even larger (19 points) for students from low-income families. There were no product reforms in mathematics during this period. Rather, process innovations that aligned instruction, curriculum, and professional development with common and well-known learning standards were likely to be at work. (2009, p. 5)

A mixed "good news/still much work to do" story comes from the Center on Education Policy from a project that examined testing data from the 50 states:

> As measured by percentages of students scoring proficient, gaps between subgroups have narrowed in most states at the elementary, middle, and high school levels, although in a notable minority of cases gaps have widened.... For example, the African American-white gap in 4th grade reading narrowed in 28 of the 36 states with adequate data, widened in 7 states, and showed no change in 1 state. (Chudowsky, Chudowsky, & Kober, 2009, p. 2)

Success stories for individual schools posted on a Web site hosted by the Learning First Alliance (http://www.publicschoolinsights.org) provide proof that schools can meet the challenge of high expectations as well as food for thought to support conversations about how to improve local schools. The Education Trust, an organization that has long focused attention on the need to close learning gaps, provides a similar resource as part of its *Dispelling the Myth* project. For example,

> George Hall Elementary School is located in one of the poorest parts of Mobile. In 2004, when Mobile Public Schools ordered George Hall to reorganize and restaff, fewer than 50 percent of the school's fourth-graders were performing at grade level in reading or mathematics. Since Tomlinson [the principal] and her team instituted some "structure," George Hall has become one of the highest performing elementary schools in all of Alabama, with 95 percent or more of its students meeting grade-level standards in reading and mathematics. (The Education Trust, 2009)

"Some schools have beaten the odds. They've made significant strides in narrowing the achievement gaps, attained proficiency levels that significantly exceeded the averages in their states, or improved student performance at an especially rapid pace.... These schools don't offer simple answers or easy solutions, but several common strategies emerge from their practices. They provide a rich curriculum coupled with strong, focused instruction. They have high expectations for all students. They use data to track student progress and individual student needs. And they employ purposeful professional development to improve teachers' skills." (The Education Trust, 2009)

Recognizing That Districts Must Be Part of the Solution

School districts make a difference. A district's policies and programs—as well as its culture—provide a framework that can help or hinder a school's efforts to improve. Studies about districts that have rapidly improved student achievement in many of their schools identified two key themes and some strategies that were remarkably similar across studies.

Theme #1—There was a clearly defined roadmap for district efforts. The most successful improvement efforts were systemic. Leaders looked at how the "pieces" of district structures and programs fit together and took a big picture view of these. Other words often used to describe district efforts are "coherent" and "comprehensive." Thus, while districts employed multiple strategies, these were intended to be mutually reinforcing whenever possible. In addition, the most successful districts limited improvement initiatives to a few key efforts, even though this sometimes required eliminating or taking resources away from popular programs.

Theme #2—There was a dual focus on excellence and equity. While district leaders recognized the requirement that more students meet standards, they also stressed the need for raising the bar over the long term. Finally, leaders sent a clear and unwavering message: Low expectations for any groups of students are unacceptable.

What Strategies Did the Successful Districts Implement?

Findings across several studies of rapidly improving districts were strikingly similar. Together they provide a valuable picture of how these districts improved (Cawelti & Protheroe, 2003).

There was an *increased emphasis on curriculum and instruction*. Gordon, in discussing Chicago school reform efforts, describes this as "moving instruction to center stage" (2002, p. 5). Teachers, often supported by central office staff, met to engage in planning for curriculum alignment, to develop pacing guides, and to talk about grade-to-grade articulation. In addition, many of the districts developed benchmark assessments that were used to identify problems with student mastery of content and skills at the school, classroom, and student level.

Resources were reorganized to support improvement efforts. Although adequate funding was an issue in many of the districts, all of them shifted resources to support the improvement efforts. In addition, discussions about resources were broadened past issues of dollars. Time and how staff members were used became explicit and important elements of the discussion.

There was an *assignment of accountability to the school level.* There was a clear signal from the superintendent, school board, and central office staff that principals and their teachers were to be held accountable for student learning. There would be no excuses.

Data-driven decision making was both a goal and a way of life in many of the districts studied. This typically required the development of more efficient ways to access and display data, a sometimes costly and time-consuming enterprise. Additionally, staff at all levels needed to be trained in the use of data.

Increased opportunities for staff communication and collaboration were provided. As districts recognized the need to better align the curriculum with state assessments, many of them scheduled time for teachers to collaborate on this project. Teachers reported that the discussions held as part of these efforts often resulted in a better understanding of grade-by-grade expectations for students—and the part they played in helping meet these. This not only got necessary work completed, it changed the culture of many of the schools and districts. Teachers felt as though they were being better supported in their work as professionals and were part of the larger picture of the district.

The districts profiled intentionally *used professional development to support improvement efforts*. Districts might, for example, provide training on the teaching of reading to all elementary grades teachers and principals. Both schools and districts also increased their use of less traditional approaches to professional development such as providing time for teachers to visit each others' classrooms.

The districts *intervened in schools making little progress*. This typically resulted in more control and supervision. But there were also increased and intentional efforts put in place for how the central office could better support these schools.

Timely assistance for students with academic difficulties was provided. While the districts and their schools had always attempted to address the needs of struggling students, the help provided could often have been characterized as too little, too late. This changed, with the intent being to provide on-target support long before a student fell so far behind that he might never catch up.

Finally, there was a *shift in the role of central office staff* from control and supervision to one of providing increased support and consultation for school-based efforts for all schools, not simply those that were low performing. Linked with this were systems that evaluated central office operations based on how well they provided effective support for schools.

How Dramatic Improvement Happens: Common How-To Lessons

"Creating the right environment for leaders of restructured schools will greatly increase the number of successful leaders and schools. The most critical environmental factors include the following:

- Freedom to act very differently with children who have not been successful learners previously. Schools that achieve learning with previously unsuccessful learners shun enormous temptations to let efficiency, consistency, prior relationships, staff preferences, parents, community wish lists, and political concerns trump what is best for student learning. They make big changes that work for learning even when inconvenient or uncomfortable.
- Accountability that is clear, frequently tracked, and publicly reported. If measurement systems are lacking, improving them rather than failing to monitor is the solution for success.
- Timeframes that allow plenty of time for planning changes but very short timetables to demonstrate success in targeted grades and subjects. Successful, big changes all get results fast. Results should be clear after one school year, with large leaps in the percentage of children making grade level and progress made by those furthest behind. Speedy support of successful strategies and the quick elimination of failed strategies happen only when timeframes are short. Even when work remains to improve learning in additional subjects and grades, there is little waiting and wondering whether the chosen change strategy will work, as with more incremental improvement strategies.
- Support that helps without hijacking a school's freedom to do things very differently with previously failing students is important. Financial, human resource, technical, data, and other service support from the district are critical, as is coordination among these functions when needed to allow deviations by a school in restructuring. But help should be provided with great care not to compromise changes that school leaders need to make (e.g., in the school schedule, curriculum, teaching approach, student progress monitoring)." (Excerpted from Hassel, Hassel, Arkin, Kowal, & Steiner, 2006, pp. 11-12.)

Principals' Views of District Support for School Improvement

Using the research base on effective districts, the Southern Regional Education Board (SREB) identified seven "strategies for districts that together form a systemic, coherent support for school reform" (Bottoms & Fry, 2009). High school principals were asked about their perceptions of how well their districts implemented these strategies. Their opinions could provide valuable information to jump-start conversations between district and school staff. For example, one of the strategies SREB identified is "Organize and engage the district office in support of each school"; however,

> Principals' responses indicate that their districts have not substantially redefined, realigned and engaged the district office to serve high schools in improving curriculum and instruction, raising student achievement and increasing completion rates. District offices still are more focused on management than on providing instructional leadership.... When asked about the support districts provide for school improvement, principals most often cited the provision of money, facilities and professional learning. Examples of support for specific instructional improvement programs were scant. In fact, principals mentioned that their districts provide additional resources for technology and improved facilities more often than additional staff or assistance for improving curriculum and instruction. (Bottoms & Fry, 2009, p. 21)

Download the SREB report, *The District Leadership Challenge: Empowering Principals to Improve Teaching and Learning*, at http://publications.sreb.org/2009/09V11_District_Leadership_Challenge_color.pdf

Focusing on Principal Leadership

What districts can do to support rapid and significant school improvement is only part of the picture. Crucial conversations must also focus directly on schools and, especially, on principal leadership. Two areas related to principal leadership are important themes for crucial conversations:

- What do school leaders that have helped low-performing schools to turn around actually *do*?
- What can districts do to support principals in school improvement efforts?

There is a strong—and growing—base of literature on the importance of principal leadership and what this looks like. Effective principals do more than support the status quo; they also support their schools in a process of continuous improvement.

But there has been recent interest in a subset of this issue. Specifically, what do the actions of principals that lead successful school turnarounds look like? Some schools may need "more dramatic change to become successful, change that looks different from incremental improvement over time" (Rhim, Kowal, Hassel, & Hassel, 2007, p. 14) and thus requires some special leadership skills. While the research base is small, it can help to inform district discussions about expectations of and support for principals in schools with a substantial need to improve.

> "School leaders who are effective in restructured schools are different from leaders who are successful maintaining and improving already high-performing schools. Successful start-up school leaders resemble entrepreneurs, and successful turnaround leaders combine the characteristics of entrepreneurs and traditional principals. Identifying and nurturing leaders capable of leading successfully in the differing restructuring environments is clearly a need for the future. But these leaders do not do everything themselves: They motivate teachers, other staff, students, and parents to higher levels of performance. They utilize the talents of staff, external consultants, and others to balance their own strengths and get the job done." (Hassel et al., 2006, p. 12)

Rhim, Kowal, Hassel, and Hassel found that leaders of successful turnarounds—both inside and outside education—concentrated on achieving a few tangible wins in year one, and that "a striking element of the research on turnarounds is that successful turnaround leaders use speedy, focused results as a major lever to change the organization's culture" (2007, p. 15). In addition, "turnarounds necessitated significant . . . changes that require a willingness to alter the basic organizational systems in place" (2007, p. 16). An example for schools might be a radical change in the way the school schedule is developed as well as what it looks like.

In their study of turnarounds in schools, Brinson, Kowal, and Hassel found that a strategy used by their principals was "focus on successful tactics; halt others" (2008, p. 6); these leaders were:

> quick to discard tactics that do not work and spend more resources and time on tactics that work. This pruning and growing process focuses limited time and money where they will have the most impact on critical results. (2008, p. 6)

These researchers also found that, in schools experiencing rapid and significant improvement, the school leaders were:

> focused on accomplishing the most *critical, consistent success actions*. While these "wins" are limited in scope, they are high-priority, not peripheral, elements of organization performance. (2008, p. 5)

Such an approach stands in sharp contrast to one often seen in less successful schools, an approach researchers at the Consortium for Chicago School Research characterize as "Christmas tree" innovations (Newmann, Smith, Allensworth, & Bryk, 2001). While such innovations may be viewed initially as addressing a problem, not all have the anticipated positive impact. Schools that do not carefully monitor and "prune" initiatives not having the desired result pull resources away from more promising possibilities. In addition, a Christmas tree full of initiatives often contributes to a lack of coherence in a school's instructional program.

Brinson, Kowal, and Hassel identified several other actions characteristic of turnaround leaders. For example,

- Initially, turnaround leaders personally analyze data about the organization's performance to identify high-priority problems that can be fixed quickly. Later, they establish organization routines that include ongoing data analysis.
- Turnaround leaders make an action plan so that everyone involved knows specifically what they need to do differently. This allows people to focus on changing what they do, rather than worrying about impending change.

- When a turnaround leader implements an action plan, change is mandatory, not optional.
- Turnaround leaders use various tactics to help staff empathize with—or "put themselves in the shoes of"—those whom they serve. This helps staff feel the problems that the status quo is causing and feel motivated to change.
- Turnaround leaders silence critics with speedy success. Early, visible wins are used not just for success in their own right, but to make it harder for others to oppose further change. This reduces leader time spent addressing "politics" and increases time spent managing for results.
- Turnaround leaders require all decision makers to share data. [This allows them] to hold staff who make key decisions accountable for results, creating discomfort for those who do not make needed changes and providing kudos to those who are achieving success. This shifts the focus of the organization's meetings from power plays, blaming, and excuses to problem solving. (2008, pp. 6-7)

These characteristics send a message to school districts—principals selected to lead a turnaround effort will need a special skill set and, in addition, special supports from their districts. For example, successful turnaround leaders talk about the importance of being able to select their own staff—and to replace staff if necessary. Another support for these principals might be the resources needed to hire someone to handle administrative tasks that are typically part of a principal's responsibilities so the principal can devote more time and attention to instructional leadership and the change process.

> Public Impact has developed a Competencies for Turnaround Success Series "designed to help district officials identify and hire the right leaders and teachers for this demanding role. These resources clarify the most critical competencies—or patterns of thinking, feeling, speaking and acting—that enable people to be successful in attempts to transform schools from failure to excellence quickly and dramatically." Guides describing the "most critical turnaround competencies" for principals and teachers as well as "toolkits for use by districts" are available. The toolkits include "detailed levels of increasingly effective competence, selection questions, guidance on how to conduct interviews that reveal information about competencies, and scoring rubrics."
>
> Download at http://www.publicimpact.com/act-strategically-when-schools-fail/competencies-for-turnaround-success

Making Hard Decisions About Persistently Low-Performing Schools

School success stories—as well as the research about them—provide strong support for conversations about how to improve schools. But the challenge for a district with a low-performing school must begin with deciding what path to take. For schools designated as persistantly low-achieving by the U.S. Department of Education's guidelines, districts are required to address the problem through one of four "allowable intervention models: transformation, turnaround, restart, and closure" (Center on Innovation & Improvement, 2010, p. 2).

Conversations about which route to take are critical. The Center for Innovation & Improvement (CII) provides a context for this conversation:

> The chief question to answer in determining the most appropriate intervention model is: What improvement strategy will result in the most immediate and substantial improvement in learning and school success for the students now attending this school *given the existing capacity in the school and the district*? There is no "correct" or "formulaic" answer to this question. Rather, relative degrees of performance and capacity should guide decision making. (2010, p. 17)

In addition, CII provides a "checklist" of school characteristics that should be assessed and discussed—and so become part of the decision-making process:

School Performance

- ❑ All students experiencing low achievement/graduation rates
- ❑ Select sub-groups of students experiencing low-performance
- ❑ Students experiencing low-achievement in all core subject areas
- ❑ Students experiencing low-achievement in only select subject areas

School Capacity

- ❑ Strong existing (2 years or less) or readily available turnaround leader
- ❑ Evidence of pockets of strong instructional staff capacity
- ❑ Evidence of limited staff capacity
- ❑ Evidence of negative school culture
- ❑ History of chronic low achievement
- ❑ Physical plant deficiencies
- ❑ Evidence of response to prior reform efforts

District Capacity

- ❑ Willing to negotiate for waivers of collective bargaining agreements related to staff transfers and removals
- ❑ Capacity to negotiate with external partners/providers
- ❑ Ability to extend operational autonomy to school
- ❑ Strong charter school law
- ❑ Experience authorizing charter schools
- ❑ Capacity to conduct rigorous charter/EMO [external management organization] selection process
- ❑ Capacity to exercise strong accountability for performance

Community Capacity

- ❑ Strong community commitment to school
- ❑ Supply of external partners/providers
- ❑ Other higher performing schools in district

The above is an excerpt; the full CII checklist is available on the CII Web site as part of their "Selecting the Intervention Model and Partners" form, http://www.centerii.org/leamodel/.

Research in four districts that closed low-performing schools highlights additional elements that should be addressed in these conversations. While some of these apply only to the school closure option, others are relevant for any decision that would radically change a school:

- Consider school closure in context of a larger reform effort.
- Let data guide decision making at all stages.
- Clearly explain to the public how students will benefit.
- Avoid contentious battles with school board members.

- Provide support to students and families during transition.
- Clarify a new principal's role in transition.
- Provide staff members with clear information about next steps (Steiner, 2009).

Obviously, the decisions to take any of these radical moves to improve chronically low-performing schools and the associated work ahead for both school and district staff are difficult. But this makes conversations about how to do this effectively so important. On a positive note, the emphasis on turning around low-performing schools over the last few years has also focused attention on collecting information about strategies observed in improving schools—and this information should be part of the conversation. For example, case studies conducted by the Center on Education Policy identified "several common findings":

- All of the case study schools that raised achievement enough to exit restructuring used multiple, coordinated strategies, which they revised over time. Study participants from schools that exited restructuring typically reported using multifaceted approaches to restructuring designed specifically to address their schools' and students' needs. Furthermore, none of the participants from schools that exited restructuring said that implementing restructuring had solved all their schools' problems. Instead, these schools revisited their strategies and changed them to adapt to new needs and funding situations.
- All case study schools that exited restructuring used data frequently to make decisions about instruction and regroup students by skill level. While all of the schools we studied reported using data to make decisions about instruction, those that exited restructuring typically used data for this purpose more frequently.
- Replacing staff helped improve many schools but sometimes had unintended negative consequences. All but one of the case study schools that exited restructuring replaced some staff. Most of

these schools had a large pool of applicants, a plan or vision for the school that allowed it to overcome its past reputation as a "failing" school, support from the teachers' union to resolve any contractual issues, and effective hiring systems that did not rely on principals alone to recruit and interview applicants. About half of the case study schools that did *not* exit restructuring also replaced some staff, but many of these schools encountered difficulties. Some principals in these schools reported being unable to replace staff with qualified teachers. Others spent so much time over the summer hiring staff that they had little time to plan for the new school year and therefore got off to a rocky start. Finally, union regulations sometimes compromised successful restaffing.

- Most case study schools that did *not* exit restructuring used similar strategies but experienced setbacks or needed more time or information. Many schools lost key staff members who were supposed to implement the strategies, and some had changes in student populations that made the strategies more difficult to implement. Other schools may need more time to implement strategies—particularly those that have had insufficient time to apply strategies that have been successful after several years in other restructuring schools in their districts. (Scott, 2009, pp. 1-2)

References

Bottoms, G., & Fry, B. (2009). *The district leadership challenge: Empowering principals to improve teaching and learning*, Atlanta, GA: Southern Regional leadership Board. Retrieved from http://publications.sreb.org/2009/09V11_District_Leadership_Challenge_color.pdf

Brinson, D., Kowal, J., & Hassel, B. C. (2008). *School turnarounds: Actions and results.* Public Impact for the Center on Innovation and Improvement. Retrieved from http://www.centerii.org/survey/downloads/Turnaround%20Actions%20and%20Results%203%2024%2008%20with%20covers.pdf

Cawelti, G., & Protheroe, N. (2003). *Supporting school improvement: Lessons from districts successfully meeting the challenge.* Arlington, VA: Educational Research Service.

Center on Innovation & Improvement. (2010). *Selecting the intervention model and partners/providers for a low-achieving school: A decision-making and planning tool for the local education agency*. Retrieved from http://www.centerii.org/leamodel/

Chudowsky, N., Chudowsky, V., & Kober, N. (2009). *State test score trends through 2007-08: Are achievement gaps closing and is achievement rising for all?* Washington, DC: Center on Education Policy.

Duncan, A. (2009). Turning around the bottom 5 percent. Retrieved from http://www2.ed.gov/news/speeches/2009/06/06222009.pdf

The Education Trust. (2009). *Success stories.* Retrieved from http://www.edtrust.org/dc/resources/success-stories

Gordon, D. T. (2002, September/October). Moving instruction to center stage. *Harvard Education Letter*, 5-7.

Hassel, E. A., Hassel, B. C., Arkin, M. D., Kowal, J. M., & Steiner, L. M. (2006). *School restructuring under No Child Left Behind: What works when? A guide for education leaders.* Washington, DC: Learning Point Associates. Retrieved from http://eric.ed.gov/ERICDocs/data/ericdocs2sql/content_storage_01/0000019b/80/28/07/cb.pdf

Loveless, T. (2009). *The 2008 Brown Center report on American education: How well are American students learning?* Washington, DC: Brookings Institution. Retrieved from http://www.brookings.edu/reports/2009/0225_education_loveless.aspx

Newmann, F. M., Smith, B., Allensworth, E., & Bryk, A. S. (2001). *School instructional program coherence: Benefits and challenges.* Chicago: Consortium on Chicago School Research. Retrieved from http://ccsr.uchicago.edu/publications/p0d02.pdf

Rhim, L. M., Kowal, J. M., Hassel, B. C., & Hassel, E. A. (2007). *School turnarounds: A review of the cross-sector evidence on dramatic organizational improvement.* Public Impact for the Center on Innovation and Improvement. Retrieved from http://www.centerii.org/survey/downloads/Turnarounds-Color.pdf

Scott, C. (2009). *Improving low-performing schools: Lessons from five years of studying school restructuring under No Child Left Behind.* Washington, DC: Center on Education Policy. Retrieved from http://www.cep-dc.org/index.cfm?fuseaction=document_ext.showDocumentByID&nodeID=1&DocumentID=300

Snipe, J., Horwitz, A., Soga, K., & Casserly, M. (2008). *Beating the odds: An analysis of student performance and achievement gaps on state assessments (results from the 2006-2007 school year).* Washington, DC: Council of the Great City Schools. Retrieved from http://www.cgcs.org/publications/BTO8_Revised.pdf

U.S. Department of Education (2009, December 10). School improvement grants; Final rule. 74 *Federal Register* 236, pp. 65,617-65,659.

Whitehurst, G. R. (2009). Innovation, motherhood, and apple pie. Washington, DC: Brown Center on Education Policy and The Brookings Institution.

Chapter 5:
Charter Schools

The Talk

Charter schools do a better job educating kids than regular public schools.

The Truth

Research has found that some charters do a better job than comparable regular public schools but many others don't. There is *no* research that supports the contention that charter schools—in general—are more effective than regular schools.

But let's provide some context to the conversation before jumping ahead to details about the research findings. In only a few years, charter schools have moved to a central place in conversations about public education, with discussions about them likely to increase significantly due to the recent federal emphasis on charters as a potential lever for broad-scale school improvement. The National Charter School Research Project talks about this:

> With the Race to the Top program encouraging the expansion of charter schools as part of the effort to reform the nation's lowest-performing district schools, charters are getting a new look—

> particularly in states that now ban or severely limit them. In response, many states are considering legislation to expand the number of charter schools allowed. (2010)

However, as these results from the annual Phi Delta Kappa/Gallup Poll of the Public's Attitudes Toward the Public Schools indicate, there is confusion about them even as public interest in them has increased:

> During the last five years, Americans' approval of charter schools has increased by 15%, as almost two out of three Americans now say they favor the idea of charter schools. At the same time, Americans still don't understand charter schools. They're evenly split on whether charter schools are in fact public schools (they are) or if they can teach religion (they can't). The majority continue to believe that charter schools can charge tuition (they can't), and almost three out of four Americans believe charter schools can select the students who attend [on the basis of ability] (they can't). (Bushaw & McNee, 2009, p. 13)

Zimmer, Gill, Booker, Lavertu, Sass, and Witte characterize the discussion about charter schools as sometimes contentious, with arguments presented both in support of and against the existence of charter schools:

> Proponents contend that charter schools expand educational choices for students, increase innovation, improve student achievement, and promote healthy competition with traditional public schools. Opponents argue that charter schools lead to increased racial or ethnic stratification of students, skim the best students from traditional public schools, reduce resources for such schools, and provide no real improvement in student outcomes. (2009, p. 1)

Finally, proponents "argue that competition from charter schools can be expected to improve traditional public schools precisely because competition threatens their budgets" (Winters, 2009).

> "You really can't begrudge the top charters their success with funders and the media. But it would be nice if traditional public schools that beat the odds could share in the limelight. You just don't hear much about them…
>
> Why is that a problem? It leaves the impression that success is possible only in charter schools. It obscures the fact that the best traditional public schools, like their most successful counterparts on the charter school side, have lessons to share about what makes a school successful. And it fuels disengagement from traditional public schools, which still educate the vast majority of American children.
>
> Let's face it. The best charter schools have come to represent all charter schools. At the same time, the worst traditional public schools have come to represent all traditional public schools. That has more to do with PR than reality, and it blinds us to many critical lessons of school reform." (von Zastrow, 2010)

What Does the Charter School Universe Look Like?

Let's briefly review the "definition" of charter schools, some history about them, and their current status in terms of numbers and students served:

> Charter schools are publicly funded schools that operate outside the direct control of local school districts, under a publicly issued charter that gives them greater autonomy than other public schools have over curriculum, instruction, and operations. Their students, or the students' parents, choose the school rather than being assigned based on residential location. The first U.S. charter school opened in 1992. (Zimmer et al., 2009, p. 1)

The National Alliance for Public Charter Schools provides additional profile and trend data on charter schools and the students who attend them:

- More than 1.4 million students now attend over 4,600 public charter schools in 40 states and the District of Columbia
- 62% of public charter school students are non-white and 48% qualify for free and reduced price lunch (compared with 45% non-white and 45% free and reduced price lunch in all public schools)
- While 56% of students attend charter schools in large cities, a growing percentage of students are enrolled in charter schools in rural areas (14% compared with 11% five years ago)
- Nearly 30% of students attend charter schools with non-traditional grade configurations, such as Kindergarten through 12th grade (compared with less than 10% of non-charter school students)
- Nationally, the average public charter school has been open 5.9 years (2009a, p. 3)

Thus, charter schools currently serve just under 3% of all students enrolled in public schools. However, the current federal emphasis placed on charters may signal that momentum toward more charter schools is building.

> "As charter schools play an increasingly central role in education reform agendas across the United States, it becomes more important to have current and comprehensible analysis about how well they do educating their students." (Center for Research on Education Outcomes [CREDO], 2009a, p. 1)

Crucial Conversations

We need to shift from skimming the surface when we talk about charter schools—and from simply repeating oft-heard statements of either proponents or critics of charter schools—to having a meaningful conversation that focuses on a more thoughtful study of the facts. The charter school "experience" has generated a good deal of data that could be helpful to discussions of school and district improvement. Let's look at some "conversation" topics that could build from this information:

- Assess the student achievement evidence concerning charters vs. traditional public schools.
- Review other impacts of charter schools on students and other public schools.
- Learn from reasons why some families and staff members have chosen charter schools.
- Ask if the greater flexibility available to charter schools might be made available to other schools.

Assess the Student Achievement Evidence Concerning Charters vs. Traditional Public Schools

A good place to begin in a conversation about charter schools is to ask: What does the research say about charter school performance? Clearly, conversations would be affected by whether charter schools in general are demonstrating a significant achievement advantage—or whether they are lagging behind their traditional public school counterparts.

But it turns out that—as with much of education research—addressing that question is not always easy. Research that compares charter school performance with that of traditional public schools (TPS in the shorthand of some researchers) is complex from several perspectives. For example, "it is virtually impossible to describe the 'typical' charter high school" (Yatsko, Gross, & Christensen, 2009, p. 5). Researchers Frankenberg, Siegel-Hawley, and Wang discuss other difficulties associated with conducting research that compares charters to TPS:

> Broad discrepancies in state charter laws, achievement tests and metrics make large-scale analyses or comparisons of outcomes difficult. A charter school in one state may operate and select students under very different regulations and incentives than a charter school in another state. Many achievement studies deal with a specific locale, resulting in a more nuanced understanding of that geographic area, but one that is not necessarily generalizeable to understanding the larger relationship between charter schools and improved student outcomes. A second issue in the achievement literature emerges due to selection bias, or the concern that students who self-select into charter or choice programs are not a random sample of all public school students. In other words, charter school attendees are not comparable to their public school peers in a basic but difficult-to-measure way. (Frankenberg, Siegel-Hawley, & Wang, 2010, p. 13)

Finally, the National Alliance for Public Charter Schools also talks about the impact on research of achievement "outliers" within the charter school population:

> It is important to note that there are a small but impressive number of public charter schools and networks of charter schools that are dramatically exceeding academic expectations.

> At the same time, there are a small but depressing number of public charter schools performing at the bottom of the heap. Any study that looks at state-wide or city-wide average student performance will not adequately capture these outliers. (2009b, p. 2)

Research Findings on Student Achievement

The bottom line—some charters do better than traditional public schools, some not as well, and most of them have similar achievement outcomes. Stanford University's Center for Research on Education Outcomes (CREDO), with the cooperation of 15 states and the District of Columbia, used longitudinal student achievement data to create "a national pooled analysis of the impact of charter schooling on student learning gains" (2009a, p. 1):

> For each charter school student, a virtual twin is created based on students who match the charter student's demographics, English language proficiency, and participation in special education or subsidized lunch programs. Virtual twins were developed for 84 percent of all the students in charter schools. The resulting matched longitudinal comparison is used to test whether students who attend charter schools fare better than if they had instead attended traditional public schools in their community. (CREDO, 2009a, p. 1)

CREDO's analysis found a "wide variation in performance" among charter schools compared to the traditional public schools:

> The study reveals that a decent fraction of charter schools, 17 percent, provide superior education opportunities for their students. Nearly half of the charter schools nationwide have results that are no different from the local public school options

> and over a third, 37 percent, deliver learning results that are significantly worse than their students would have realized had they remained in traditional public schools. (CREDO, 2009a, p. 1)

CREDO also found that geographic patterns existed—five states in which charter schools produced higher learning gains than traditional schools, six with lower than average gains, and four states with mixed results or gains that were similar between the two groups. In addition, the researchers found that, on average:

> Charter students in elementary and middle school grades have significantly higher rates of learning than their peers in traditional public schools, but students in charter high schools and charter multi-level schools have significantly worse results. Charter schools have different impacts on students based on their family backgrounds. For Blacks and Hispanics, their learning gains are significantly worse than that of their traditional school twins. However, charter schools are found to have better academic growth results for students in poverty. English Language Learners realize significantly better learning gains in charter schools. Students in Special Education programs have about the same outcomes. Students do better in charter schools over time. First year charter students on average experience a decline in learning, which may reflect a combination of mobility effects and the experience of a charter school in its early years. Second and third years in charter schools see a significant reversal to positive gains. (2009a, p. 6)

After a review critical of the technical approach CREDO took was issued by another Stanford researcher, Carolyn Hoxby (2009), CREDO (2009b) responded with a defense of the statistical approach taken. The federal What Works Clearinghouse then reviewed the CREDO study and found it to be "consistent with WWC standards with reservations," stating:

> Although the study matched charter school students to traditional public school students based on demographic characteristics and test scores, it is possible that there were other differences between the two groups that were not accounted for in the analysis, and these differences could have influenced achievement growth. (2010)

An eight-state study by RAND found that "charter middle and high schools produce test score achievement gains that are, on average, similar to those of traditional public schools" (Zimmer et al., 2009, p. 1). Finally, Betts and Tang reviewed the literature on charter schools and point to a "lack of rigorous studies" (2008, p. 1). Using only the 13 studies they identified as rigorous, they reanalyzed data and found mixed results:

> two cases in which charter schools appear quite frequently to outperform traditional public schools are elementary school reading and middle school math, although the effect sizes are small in the latter case. Conversely, charter schools often significantly underperform in high school reading and math. (2008, p. 1)

In addition to these overview studies, it can be helpful to review those focused on a narrow geographic area. For example, Raymond talks about a CREDO study of charter schools in New York City:

> [In New York City], the average student in a charter school learns significantly more in both reading and math than the average student in a traditional public school. Not only were charter schools as a whole better in New York than in any other city we have studied; there also was less range in quality. Although there were some underperforming charter schools in New York City, they made up a far smaller proportion of the whole than in California or the rest of the nation. (2010)

In contrast, charter schools in Minnesota were studied by the Institute on Race and Poverty. The report authors found that "although a few charter schools perform well," "charter schools in Minnesota still perform worse on average than comparable traditional public schools" (2008, p. 1).

Review Other Impacts of Charter Schools on Students and Other Public Schools

While student achievement should obviously be the key indicator when comparing charter to traditional public schools, a crucial conversation should also take a broader view of outcomes and then ask what the results might mean for other public schools. For example, the eight-state study conducted by RAND found that "charter high school students had a higher probability of graduating and attending college" (Zimmer et al., 2009, p. 1). Booker, Sass, Gill, and Zimmer focused their research on charter high schools in Florida and Chicago. While controlling for student demographics, they found "the estimated impact of attending a charter high school on the probability of obtaining a high school diploma is positive in both Florida and Chicago" (2010).

In addition,

> among the study population of charter 8th graders, students who attended a charter high school in 9th grade are 8 to 10 percentage points more likely to attend college than similar students who attended a traditional public high school. (2010)

Winters (2009) talks about the "collateral effects" of charters on traditional public schools, and research is also beginning to provide information about these. For example, the eight-state study by RAND found that:

> - Charter schools do not generally draw the top students away from traditional public schools.
> - [There is] no evidence that charter schools substantially affect achievement in nearby traditional public schools. (Zimmer et al., 2009, p. 1)

However, the RAND study also found variation among states, thus emphasizing how important it is to conduct more localized studies.

Concerns About Segregation

Some opponents of charters schools, as well as some researchers, express concern that charter schools may be increasing racial and/or economic segregation in both the charters themselves and the traditional public schools from which they draw students. This clearly could be the topic of a crucial conversation, one that might piggyback on one some districts are already having about the student mix in their schools.

A study conducted by The Civil Rights Project at UCLA addressed this issue. Researchers analyzed federal data on charter school enrollment from 40 states, the District of Columbia, and several metropolitan areas and found that:

> Charter schools are more racially isolated than traditional public schools in virtually every state and large metropolitan area in the nation. While there are examples of charter schools with vibrant diversity, this report shows these schools to be the exception. (Frankenberg et al., 2010, p. 80)

The researchers go on to identify some major themes from their analysis:

> Charter schools attract a higher percentage of black students than traditional public schools, in part because they tend to be located in urban areas.... While segregation for blacks among all public schools has been increasing for nearly two decades, black students in charter schools are far more likely than their traditional public school counterparts to be educated in intensely segregated settings....
>
> Charter school trends vary substantially across different regions of the country. Latinos are under-enrolled in charter schools in some Western states where they comprise the largest share of students. At the same time, a dozen states (including those with high concentrations of Latino students like Arizona and Texas) report that a majority of Latino charter students attend intensely segregated minority schools. Patterns in the West and in a few areas in the South, the two most racially diverse regions of the country, also suggest that charters serve as havens for white flight from public schools. Finally, in the industrial Midwest, more students enroll in charter schools compared to other regions, and Midwestern charter programs display high concentrations of black students. (Frankenberg et al., 2010, pp. 4-5)

The researchers also express concern that "major gaps in multiple federal data sources make it difficult to answer basic, fundamental questions about the extent to which charter schools enroll and concentrate low-income students and English Language Learners (ELLs)" (2010, p. 5).

There have also been special concerns about segregation of students—students of color, ELLs, poor students, and special education students—in schools operated by Education Management Organizations (EMOs), 95% of which are charter schools. A report issued by the Education and Public Interest Center suggests this concern might have some merit:

- Charter schools operated by EMOs tend to be strongly racial segregative for both minority and majority students as compared with the composition of the sending district. Only one-fourth of the charter schools had a composition relatively similar to that of the sending district.
- For economically challenged students, EMO-operated charter schools more strongly segregate students than do their respective local districts. The student population is pushed out to the extremes. Most charter schools were divided into either very segregative high-income schools or very segregative low-income schools. Between 70% and 73% of the schools were in the extreme categories of the scale, depending on the comparison.
- EMO-operated schools consistently enrolled a lower proportion of special education children than their home district. Past research has shown that charter schools have less capacity for special education children. Thus, parents tended to select away (or were counseled away) from charter schools. A small group of charter schools focused on special needs children and were, consequently, highly segregative in this regard.

- English Language Learners (ELL) were also consistently underrepresented in charter schools in every comparison. While one-third of the EMO schools had an ELL population similar to the sending district, the distribution was highly skewed, with well over half the EMO schools being segregated. (Miron, Urshel, Mathis, & Tornquist, 2010, pp. i-ii)

Learn From Reasons Why Some Families and Staff Members Have Chosen Charter Schools

"Though there are exceptions, most school districts that have lost and continue to lose students do not respond competitively" (National Charter School Research Project, 2010). Thus, looking at why families and staff choose charter schools—and then asking whether there are ways in which traditional public schools could become more "charter-like" while still fulfilling their mission—is important.

Over a decade ago, when charter schools were just beginning to receive attention on the national scene, researchers surveyed parents and teachers affiliated with charter schools and asked why charters were attractive to them. Parents indicated factors such as school size, a school philosophy closer to their own, increased opportunity for parent involvement, and the perception that teachers and curriculum in the charter would be better were all important to their decision to enroll their students in charters. Key reasons for teachers included: the school's educational philosophy, the opportunity to work with like-minded teachers and administrators, and small school size (Vanourek, Manno, Finn, & Bierlein, 1997).

A more recent study of charter schools by Yatsko, Gross, and Christensen (2009) focused on characteristics found in many of them. Several of these highlight reasons why charter schools are attractive to students, their families, or staff, such as the fact they:

- Often have more focused and strategic missions, serving either a specific subgroup of students or focusing on a specific type of instruction.
- Are more likely to tailor instructional approaches and curriculum to individual student needs, for example, by having a cultural focus or by providing special supports for struggling students.
- Are more likely to focus on college preparation even in schools serving heavily minority, low-income student populations.
- Have a tendency to actively seek out teachers with the ability to connect with students, with schools able to "take advantage of the flexibility they had in certification and job description to look beyond the traditional pool of certified education school graduates" (2009, p. 11).
- Aggressively structure conditions of employment, for example, by "experimenting with compensation and contractual arrangements that value performance over tenure" (p. 13) and, also, by "capitalizing on teachers' outside interests" (p. 13).
- Use small and relationship-based schools to build community.
- Experiment with unusual grade and administrative configurations, such as high schools expanding the grades served downward or a "flattening out of the administrative team by distributing key leadership tasks and decisions to interested and capable teachers" (p. 16).

Tom Fowler-Finn, formerly superintendent of the Cambridge (MA) public school district talks about the need for public school districts to do a better job marketing its schools:

> Not one charter school I've seen comes close to the comprehensive intellectual stimulation and programming offered by strong public school systems. The public often does not realize this. For example, the course offerings and extracurriculars at Cambridge Rindge and Latin School, the public high school in Cambridge, Mass., are incomparable and marketable. They include courses in world languages and culture, the arts, advanced academic course options, and extracurriculars and varsity sports. In fact, we only recently realized the significant advantage we had in promoting the quality of our facilities.... A community survey revealed the pulling power of our facilities today, a surprise to us until we recognized the lack of such facilities in charter schools. (2008)

Ask If the Greater Flexibility Available to Charter Schools Might Be Made Available to Other Schools

In her work on charter schools, Lake asks "How can charters prompt district improvement?" She goes on to talk about this issue:

> Districts that steadfastly refuse to revamp their schools in the face of charter or other competition are not all alike. Districts with growing student populations might not care if they lose some enrollment to charter schools. Other districts are feeling real competitive pressure from charter schools, but either do not know how to respond or are frozen in place by local politics. Some complain that charters have unfair advantages and assert that their districts don't have the flexibility to compete

> effectively. A growing number of districts are, in fact, trying to compete, but in failing to understand why parents leave and what makes successful charter schools tick, they cannot respond effectively. (Lake, 2010, p. 50)

She goes on to urge school districts to be more open-minded about the issue of charter schools—moving from simply viewing them as a threat to studying them for information about what a district or its schools could do differently:

> While it is true that charter school performance is often inconsistent, district personnel are foolish to believe they cannot learn something from charters. In almost every state, the charter sector is producing examples of schools that are achieving breakthrough results that most districts cannot replicate and that cannot be explained away by student selection. Long wait lists and parent satisfaction ratings demonstrate that charter schools often offer something that is less easily measured by test scores, but may be equally important to students and parents.
>
> Finally, it is clear that, in order to compete effectively, districts need to build new central office capacities and develop a better understanding of what makes successful charter schools work. (Lake, 2010, pp. 53-54)

One component of what makes successful charter schools work is the flexibility they are permitted. There are clearly elements of some charter schools that might be difficult—although perhaps not impossible—for traditional public schools to put in place with the current level of available resources. For example, Education Sector (2009) points to the extra instructional time provided to students in the KIPP program as compared to traditional public schools—

possibly 60% more time each year. However, not all changes require additional resources. School districts should assess their own policies and procedures and ask whether modifying some of them—or at least making it possible for a school to request a waiver—might help a school more effectively address its students' needs. Another route might be working with other school districts to make the case to the state education agency that changes in specific state requirements might support school efforts.

In a study of charter schools in Indiana, Plucker highlights some areas in which charters have been able to innovate due to increased flexibility:

> Charter schools utilize flexibility in staffing, class size, curriculum, and teaching materials decisions and in the length of school days and school years. Charter schools are able to be somewhat more flexible in adapting and changing curriculum (although all school corporations may request waivers to do the same). Several charter schools have changed their school calendar or their instructional programs—often utilizing calendars and schedules that lengthen the school day or add instructional time to the day itself. (2008, p. 13)

In addition, the previously mentioned Yatsko, Gross, and Christensen (2009) study already highlighted an option some charter schools have that is not available to most traditional public schools—the ability to adjust the approach to teacher compensation and to easily remove under-performing teachers.

References

Betts, J. R., & Tang, Y. E. (2008). *Value-added and experimental students of the effects of charter schools on student achievement: A literature review.* Seattle, WA: National Charter School Research Project, Center on Reinventing Public Education, University of Washington Bothell. Retrieved from http://www.crpe.org/cs/crpe/download/csr_files/pub_ncsrp_bettstang_dec08.pdf

Booker, K., Sass, T. R., Gill, B., & Zimmer, R. (2010, Spring). The unknown world of charter high schools. *Education Next*. Retrieved from http://educationnext.org/the-unknown-world-of-charter-high-schools/

Bushaw, W. J., & McNee, J. A. (2009, September). Americans speak out. Are educators and policy makers listening? The 41st annual Phi Delta Kappa/Gallup poll of the public's attitudes toward the public schools. *Phi Delta Kappan*, 9-23.

Center for Research on Education Outcomes. (2009a). *Multiple choice: Charter school performance in 16 states.* Stanford, CA: Author. Retrieved from http://credo.stanford.edu/reports/MULTIPLE_CHOICE_CREDO.pdf

Center for Research on Education Outcomes. (2009b*). CREDO finale to Hoxby's revised memorandum*. Stanford, CA: Author. Retrieved from http://credo.stanford.edu/reports/CREDO%20Finale%20to%20Hoxby.pdf

Education Sector. (2009). *Growing pains: Scaling up the nation's best charter schools*. Retrieved from http://www.educationsector.org/usr_doc/Growing_Pains.pdf

Fowler-Finn, T. (2008, May). Charter schools uncovered: What we learned through our own analysis about the skewed comparisons between our schools and the local charters. *School Administrator*, pp. 34-37.

Frankenberg, E., Siegel-Hawley, G., & Wang, J. (2010). *Choice without equity: Charter school segregation and the need for civil rights standards.* Los Angeles, CA: The Civil Rights Project/Proyecto Derechos Civiles at UCLA. Retrieved from http://www.civilrightsproject.ucla.edu/news/pressreleases/CRP-Choices-Without-Equity-report.pdf

Hoxby, C. M. (2009). *A statistical mistake in the CREDO study of charter schools.* Retrieved from http://credo.stanford.edu/reports/memo_on_the_credo_study%20II.pdf

Institute on Race and Poverty. (2008). Failed promises: Assessing charter schools in the Twin Cities. Retrieved from http://www.irpumn.org/uls/resources/projects/2_Charter_Report_Final.pdf

Lake, R. J. (2010). Achieving the ripple effect: How can charters prompt district improvement? In R. J. Lake (Ed.), *Hopes, fears, and reality: A balanced look at American charter schools in 2009* (pp. 49-56). Seattle, WA: Center on Reinventing Public Education, University of Washington. Retrieved from http://www.crpe.org/cs/crpe/view/csr_pubs/306

Miron, G., Urshel, J. L., Mathis, W. J., & Tornquist, E. (2010). *Schools without diversity: Education management organizations, charter schools, and the demographic stratification of the American school system*. Boulder, CO and Tempe, AZ: Education and the Public Interest Center. Retrieved from http://epicpolicy.org/files/EMO-Seg.pdf

National Alliance for Public Charter Schools. (2008). *Charter school executives: Toward a new generation of leadership*. Washington, DC: National Alliance for Public Charter Schools. Retrieved from http://www.publiccharters.org/files/publications/2008_Toward%20a%20New%20Generation%20of%20Leadership.pdf

National Alliance for Public Charter Schools. (2009a). *Public charter school dashboard 2009*. Washington, DC: Author. Retrieved from http://www.publiccharters.org/files/publications/DataDashboard.pdf

National Alliance for Public Charter Schools. (2009b). *Charter school achievement: What we know* (5th edition). Washington, DC: Author. Retrieved from http://www.publiccharters.org/files/publications/Summary%20of%20Achievement%20Studies%20Fifth%20Edition%202009_Final.pdf

National Charter School Research Project. (2010). *Hopes, fears, & reality: A balanced look at American charter schools in 2009* (Overview). Retrieved from http://www.crpe.org/cs/crpe/view/csr_pubs/306

Plucker, J. (2008). *Study of the effectiveness and efficiency of charter schools in Indiana*. Bloomington, IN: Center for Evaluation and Education Policy. Retrieved from http://ceep.indiana.edu/projects/PDF/ExecutiveSummaryHEA1001-2007.pdf

Raymond, M. E. (2010, February 1). L.A. could learn a lot about charter schools from the Big Apple. *Los Angeles Times*. Retrieved from http://articles.latimes.com/2010/feb/01/opinion/la-oe-raymond1-2010feb01

Vanourek, G., Manno, B. V., Finn, C. E., & Bierlein, L. A. (1997). *Charter schools as seen by those who know them best: Students, teachers, and parents*. Washington, DC: Hudson Institute.

von Zastrow, K. (2010). *Can traditional public schools share the limelight with charters?* Retrieved from http://www.publicschoolinsights.org/can-traditional-public-schools-share-limelight-charters

What Works Clearinghouse. (2010). *WWC quick review of the report "Multiple Choice: Charter School Performance in 16 States."* Washington, DC: Author. Retrieved from http://ies.ed.gov/ncee/wwc/publications/quickreviews/QRReport.aspx?QRID=137

Winters, M. A. (2009, October). Everyone wins: How charter schools benefit all New York City public school students. *Civic Report*. Retrieved from http://www.manhattan-institute.org/html/cr_60.htm

Yatsko, S., Gross, B., & Christensen, J. (2009). *Charter high schools: Alternative paths to graduation*. Seattle, WA: Center on Reinventing Public Education. Retrieved from http://www.crpe.org/cs/crpe/download/csr_files/whp_ics_altpaths_nov09.pdf

Zimmer, R., Gill, B., Booker, K., Lavertu, S., Sass, T. R., & Witte, J. (2009). *Are charter schools making a difference?: A study of student outcomes in eight states.* (RAND Research Brief). Santa Monica, CA: RAND. Retrieved from http://www.rand.org/pubs/research_briefs/2009/RAND_RB9433.pdf

Chapter 6:
Pay for Performance

The Talk

Kids suffer because poor teachers make the same pay as good teachers. Why hasn't public education learned from business?

The Truth

The concept of differentiated pay strikes a responsive chord because of its commonsense appeal that more productive workers should be paid more. But a key question should be—does an incentive pay approach impact student achievement? RAND Education reviewed research from both inside and outside the U.S. and concluded that "overall, there is insufficient evidence to support claims that [pay for performance] will improve achievement in the United States" (Hamilton & Li, 2009, p. 1).

However, the current discussion about incentive pay makes it clear that the issue is broader than has been measured to date by research projects attempting to link the practice with student learning outcomes. For example, a pay for performance component of compensation is often used in the private sector and is part of the experience of many workers. Thus, paying "bad" teachers as much as "good" ones sometimes creates a public relations problem for public education:

> The public feels the teacher compensation structure rewards mediocrity; changing teacher compensation can reassure the public that we value teacher performance. In the minds of many of the public, teachers earn more pay just for sticking around and taking more classes.... With education budgets under scrutiny, there will be a push to find better, more effective, and more efficient ways to use teacher salary dollars. (Odden, 2000)

In addition, the issue of how teachers are paid is much more important than its impact on public relations. Implicit in many of the discussions about changes to the teacher compensation system is the potential of money as a motivator. Hassel suggests salaries—both their levels and the ways compensation is structured—have a significant impact on teachers:

> The way we pay affects the behavior of teachers: how they teach and how they develop their teaching capabilities over time. How they choose to direct their energies—inside the classroom and out—will in part be driven by what kinds of practices and capacity-building habits are rewarded by the pay system. (2002, p. 4)

"Pay matters. It has an impact on who decides to stay and who goes looking for greener pastures. Compensation systems signal what skills and attributes are valued and what kinds of contributions reap rewards." (National Commission on Teaching and America's Future, 2003, p. 29)

Periodically since the single salary schedule that is the tradition in public K-12 education became the norm, interest in replacing it—or at least supplementing it with provisions that address teacher performance or skills—has been expressed by politicians, members of the general public, and some educators. However, this time seems to be different:

> In U.S. education policy, it is quite common for reform ideas to cycle in and back out of the spotlight. One such reform is incentive pay for educators. Recently, this reform has secured itself firmly at the top of the education policy agenda and in the public eye. (Heyburn, Lewis, & Ritter, 2010, p. 1)

Over the past decade, interest in teacher salaries—how much they are paid and how their pay is determined—has reached a new high. There are several reasons for both the resurgence of interest and the tenacity with which this reform effort is now taking hold. First, an increasing number of states and districts—some with the involvement of organizations such as the Milken Family Foundation that supported development of the Teacher Advancement Program (TAP)—have implemented structures that shift away from dependence on the traditional salary schedule. Second, research that attempts to link specific teachers to student growth has both developed more sophisticated methods for doing this and, perhaps more important, produced statistical evidence of the impact—positive or negative—that one teacher can have on a student's learning. Goldhaber talks about this research:

> More recent research utilizing datasets that link individual teachers to their individual students is yielding new insights about how teachers compare to one another. This work shows that there is tremendous variation in the effectiveness of teachers in the workforce (measured based on their value-added contribution toward student achievement). (2008, p. 4)

A third factor has been the major push for incentive pay in the last few years from the national level. The federal Teacher Incentive Fund (TIF) was originally authorized in 2006. Prior to 2010, TIF supported 33 grant sites, with implementation in 109 school districts, including a few charter school districts. An additional round of funding—to a total of approximately $439 million—has been authorized for fiscal year 2010:

> The grants are intended to support projects that develop and implement performance-based compensation systems (PBCSs) for teachers and principals in order to increase educator effectiveness and student achievement in high-need schools. Applicants must use TIF funds to develop and implement PBCSs that at a minimum—
>
> (a) Consider gains in student academic achievement as well as classroom evaluations conducted multiple times during each school year among other factors, and
>
> (b) Provide educators with incentives to take on additional responsibilities and leadership roles. (U.S. Department of Education, 2010)

In addition, the U.S. Department of Education funds the Center for Educator Compensation Reform (CECR), an organization charged with working to raise national awareness of alternative strategies for educator compensation (www.cecr.ed.gov). Finally, teacher opposition to differentiated pay—previously especially strong in regard to pay for performance—seems to be moderating, although it is definitely still a force in the discussion.

Pay for performance is often presented as an easy fix to improve the quality of teaching. Lavy talks about this:

> The quest to improve public education has led policymakers and researchers to focus on how to increase teachers' effectiveness. One obvious means is compensation. According to many observers, the traditional basis for teacher pay—years of service and education—provides little incentive for excellence. To make teachers more effective, these critics argue, pay should be tied to performance. (2007, p. 88)

However, pay for performance is only one salary issue that should be included in conversations about ways to improve public education. The broader focus should be on how we hire and retain good teachers, with attention given to ensuring that all students achieve high levels of learning. The Consortium for Policy Research in Education emphasizes the importance of taking that view of the issue:

> Teacher compensation is a critical element of a human resources management system, and should be designed to work together with other elements of the system (e.g., organizational goals, professional development, principal leadership, teacher recruitment and selection) to enhance school performance. (n.d.)

Crucial Conversations

So it's time for school leaders to intentionally focus a crucial conversation on the broad topic of teacher compensation. Goldhaber would agree with the importance of this issue, since in his view,

> Few school systems strategically use compensation as a policy tool to achieve various objectives: a fairer allocation of teacher quality across students, hiring and keeping teachers with key knowledge and skills, and increasing student achievement via measurable results. (2009, p. 1)

As part of the conversation, key elements should be addressed; among these are:

- Supporting the goal of an excellent teacher in every classroom through teacher compensation.
- Engaging teachers in conversations about what matters to them.
- Focusing on implementation issues involved with shifting to a new approach to teacher compensation.

Pay for Performance: Some Key Issues

In a policy brief developed for the Obama administration, RAND Education outlined some key points on what is known about pay for performance (called P4P by RAND) in K-12 education:

"P4P programs have led to higher student achievement in some cases, but the research is limited. There are few studies of the effects of P4P on student achievement, and some of the best evidence comes from other countries and therefore may not apply to education in the United States.... Overall, there is insufficient evidence to support claims that P4P will improve achievement in the United States.

Attaching stakes to test scores leads to changes in curricula and instruction. When tests are used to reward or penalize schools or individual educators, teachers and administrators tend to respond by focusing more on tested material and less on material not tested. These changes may be positive if educators spend more time on more-important topics, but the changes may also be undesirable if they take time away from valued subjects or result in excessive focus on a narrow set of test items.

(continued on next page)

The data needed to measure achievement gains or estimate added value are not always available. Most P4P programs evaluate teachers or principals using student test scores while controlling for prior achievement. Researchers are developing more and better methods for evaluating the value of P4P programs, but the measures work only with annual, consecutive-grade testing. Adopting P4P in early elementary grades, high school, and subjects other than reading and mathematics tends to be much more difficult because of a lack of such testing.

The contribution of a single teacher is difficult to measure. In most schools, multiple teachers and other staff interact with students and may influence their performance, which is one reason school-level incentives are sometimes preferred over individual teacher incentives. In addition, it is important to recognize that factors outside the school also influence student achievement.

Measures of teaching or leadership practices may lead to better professional development and increase educators' acceptance of the program.…Findings from the limited studies available suggest that measuring teaching or leadership practices allows supervisors to provide useful feedback to teachers and principals, and it may increase educators' support for the program.

We know little about the effects of P4P on school climate and staff morale. Research suggests that teacher and principal support for a reform, as well as an environment of collaboration and trust, is important to its success. However, there is little evidence about how P4P affects the school environment.

We still lack evidence-based guidance for designing effective P4P programs. A number of choices must be made when adopting P4P. These include what subjects to include, how to address teachers who do not teach tested subjects, how (and whether) to reward principals in addition to teachers, and whether to reward groups (e.g., a school's entire staff) or individuals. There are also questions about how best to deal with students for whom existing tests may not provide valid information—e.g., English-language learners and students with disabilities." (Excerpt from Hamilton & Li, 2009, pp. 1-2.)

Supporting the Goal of an Excellent Teacher in Every Classroom Through Teacher Compensation

Hassel and Hassel highlight the importance of a district's compensation structure to the goal of an excellent teacher in every classroom:

> Pay is not just about dollars. The structure of pay—who is paid how much and for what—sends a strong signal about whether teaching is a profession where high achievement and high achievers are valued. (2007, p. 3)

Discussion that broadens the picture of the structure of compensation past the traditional salary schedule that rewarded primarily education and experience makes sense. First, Goldhaber reports on research that found "only about 3 percent of the contribution teachers made to student learning was associated with teacher experience, degree attained, and other readily observable characteristics" (2002). Second, the traditional schedule fails to address issues such as the difficulty in attracting and retaining science and math teachers or teachers for schools serving high numbers of at-risk students.

Thus, a more comprehensive discussion about teacher compensation needs to begin with district goals—such as a high-quality education for all students—and also address strategies that might help to meet these goals. Hassel and Hassel describe a variety of approaches to teacher compensation and call these generally "pay for contribution." Together these approaches provide a framework for a comprehensive discussion about teacher pay:

- **Performance pay:** significant bonus pay to teachers for gains in student learning results;
- **Hard-to-staff school pay:** additional compensation for teachers who work in high-poverty schools, and very significant performance rewards to those who contribute more to growth in student learning in these schools;
- **Skill shortage pay:** additional compensation to attract teachers in shortage areas, such as math, science, and special education, and very significant performance rewards to those who contribute more to student learning gains in the shortage areas;
- **Advanced role pay:** additional compensation for advanced or "master" teaching roles—and teachers capable of filling them—that contribute measurably more to student learning;
- **Skill and knowledge pay:** additional compensation for specific skills that lead to proven, measurable gains in student learning, particularly in states where teacher-level assessment of student gains has not been implemented;
- **Limited advanced degree pay:** additional compensation for holders of advanced degrees only in fields, such as secondary mathematics, where such degrees have a proven effect on student learning; and
- **Retention pay:** significant one-time pay boosts after the early years of teaching experience to retain higher performers. (Hassel & Hassel, 2007, p. 1)

Taking a Value-Added Approach

"While the statistical methods are complex, the definition of effective teaching is not. Simply, researchers looked for the change in students' test scores according to the teacher they were assigned to. A highly effective teacher, therefore, is one whose students show the most gains from one year to the next. By using this approach, researchers are able to isolate the effect of the teacher from other factors related to student performance, for example, students' prior academic record or school they attend." (Center for Public Education, 2006)

The Measurement Issue

Although the discussion should begin first with goals—for example, attracting the best teachers to the lowest-performing schools might be identified as a high-priority need—another component of the discussion will need to focus on the issue of who will receive special "pay for contribution." Hassel talks about this from the perspective of only one category—although probably the thorniest to address—pay for performance:

> What kind of performance should be rewarded? Should performance be defined as the proportion of students meeting a set standard, the rate of growth students achieve, a more sophisticated calculation of "value added" by a school or teacher, or a combination of these measures? Should the metric be students' scores on standardized tests, or should other indicators of student performance be part of the calculation? If other reliable indicators of student performance are in use in a school, district, or state, there is no reason why they could not be incorporated into a teacher compensation system. Should student performance be the only basis for the system, or should schools or teachers be rated on other factors as well? We tend to think of "performance" as student performance, but there is no *a priori* reason why a performance-based teacher compensation system would have to be predicated solely on student performance.... For example, a district with a teacher-mentoring program could reward mentors based in part on progress made by their "mentees" on a scale of knowledge and skills.

There are no hard and fast answers to these questions, but there are some important design principles to keep in mind. The first almost goes without saying: Whatever kind of "performance" is rewarded should be something that is *highly valued* by the

> school, district, or state. This principle argues for including student performance in the system, or for ensuring that any nonstudent indicators are closely linked to valued student outcomes. But there is no reason why performance has to be defined solely in terms of student results on standardized tests. Second, performance incentives are likely to be more powerful (and more widely accepted) the more *control* an individual has over the performance variable. For example, granting performance bonuses only to teachers at schools where more than 90 percent of students meet grade-level standards is likely to provide minimal incentives for (and quite a bit of grumbling among) teachers at schools starting with fewer than 10 percent at grade level. Third, *alignment* of performance pay with the greater organizational culture and structure of a school or district is critical. If a school, for example, is seeking to foster collaboration among teachers, performance pay should not undermine such collegiality. Better yet, it should be designed to support collaboration. In this context, there is no "ideal" performance pay system—different approaches will make sense in different schools and districts. (2002, p. 25)

Individually based teacher rewards "presume an ability to accurately and fairly measure teacher effectiveness based on student test performance" (Goldhaber, 2009, p. 19). However, Goldhaber also reports that:

> Research has clearly demonstrated that it is no simple task to isolate teachers' contributions toward student achievement or to know how much student and teacher data is necessary in order to make strong inferences about the differences in performance between teachers. (2009, p. 26)

Honawar is even less positive about this required component of a pay for performance salary system tied to student outcomes:

> A handful of new studies that scrutinize performance-pay initiatives nationwide have found mixed results on how they affect student achievement. That conclusion reinforces views that more work is needed on such plans, despite a recent surge in their popularity, before they can replace the traditional single salary schedule. (2009)

However, it is likely that the momentum toward greater use of pay for performance approaches will continue. The challenge, then, is designing ways to accurately sort high-performing teachers from others. Some of the work that needs to be done is technical; thus, "ongoing improvement of student testing to measure student learning progress accurately is an important complement to pay reform" (Hassel & Hassel, 2007, p. 3). Other work—such as building the capacity to collect and use relevant data—will need to be done at the district level.

While supportive of efforts to link student learning and teacher effects, the Center for Teaching Quality includes among its "philosophical principles" this caution:

> Student achievement data from standardized tests should not be the only measure used to gauge student success. Due to the extreme complexity of identifying high-performing teachers using student achievement data and the problems inherent in many standardized test results, additional measures need to be used when making judgments about the effectiveness of teachers. (2006)

> "$5,000 is one month's pay for me. I have 36 years of experience and a Master's plus 120 hours [class credits]. I have been at the very top of the salary schedule in my district for 11 years. $5,000 more a year would allow me to pay off my mortgage by retirement, to clean up my home improvement loan, maybe do some repairs that are needed, maybe take a vacation, buy some classroom materials, take a class. But I will not do it at the expense of my friends." (Teacher response to survey, in Goldhaber, DeArmond, & DeBurgomaster, 2007, p. 20)

Engaging Teachers in Conversations About What Matters to Them

Heneman, Milanowski, and Kimball (2007) view assessing potential teacher reaction to any change in the compensation as an important prerequisite to its introduction. Conversations with all affected parties in the district considering changes to the compensation are essential. However, these can be informed by some research-based efforts to elicit teacher opinion about both compensation and other workplace issues "such as time for planning or collaboration with peers, positive and supportive principal leadership, opportunities to influence school decision making, and adequate curricular resources have all been mentioned in the literature" (Learning Point Associates, 2007). In addition, research has recently begun to identify differences in opinions about incentive pay from among different groups of teachers—for example, those new to the profession and more experienced teachers. Understanding these differences may be important when designing incentive programs intended to reward high-performing teachers or, alternatively, to encourage teachers to serve in hard-to-staff schools. Chait and Miller provide an overview of some of the findings from teacher surveys:

> Findings point toward four key ideas. First, teachers are more likely to support performance-pay programs targeted to high-needs schools than to all schools. Second, novice or younger teachers may be more receptive to performance-pay programs than veteran teachers, which means more outreach may be needed to veteran teachers or perhaps programs should begin by including only novice teachers and allowing veteran teachers to opt in if they choose. Third, teachers are likely to be more supportive of programs that rely on a variety of measures of teacher performance rather than those that only rely on one measure. Fourth, teachers will be more supportive of performance pay if they trust their principals and therefore strong relationships between teachers and principals are an important prerequisite for successful programs. (Chait & Miller, 2009, p. 9)

When asked whether they agreed with the statement, "other teachers contribute to my success in the classroom," 91% of teachers responding to the MetLife 2009 Survey of the American Teacher said that they agreed "strongly" or "somewhat." (Harris Interactive, 2010)

Two studies conducted after the Chait and Miller analysis—one a large-scale survey of teachers at all stages of their careers and another of younger teachers—yield similar results. For example, a teacher survey conducted by Scholastic and the Bill & Melinda Gates Foundation (2010) asked 40,000 teachers to provide their views on factors that impact teacher retention:

> When asked about the things that are most important in retaining good teachers, supportive leadership, time for collaboration and a high-quality curriculum top the list, with supportive leadership by far the most important factor in teacher retention. Higher salaries fall squarely in the middle—important, but less so than non-monetary factors. Pay tied to teachers' performance…

> is the lowest-ranked item, with 36% of teachers saying it is not at all important and 25% saying it is absolutely essential or very important in retaining good teachers. (p. 39)
>
> Teachers are about three times as likely to say that higher salaries are absolutely essential or very important in retaining good teachers as they are to say the same of pay tied to performance (82% vs. 26%, respectively). Given teachers' lack of confidence in most performance measurements, this is not surprising. While teachers' support of higher salaries does not vary significantly across the key dimensions of grade level taught, years of teaching experience or school median household income, views on pay for performance do vary across some subgroups, including years of teaching experience and, to a lesser extent, school income. (p. 41)
>
> Veteran teachers are the least likely to think that pay tied to performance is either very important or absolutely essential in retaining good teachers. In conversations, teachers express concern that merit-based pay systems might discourage collaborative work, which they say positively impacts student achievement. Additionally, with collaboration being such an important factor in teachers' job satisfaction, skepticism of pay for performance is understandable. Teachers also shared their views on the impact that monetary rewards for teacher performance would have on improving student achievement. In short, about as many teachers say this would make a very strong/strong impact (28%) on improving student achievement as do those who say this would make no impact at all (30%). (p. 42)

A survey of Generation Y teachers (born between 1977 and 1995) found they are "more open to rewarding teachers differentially for their performance and responsibilities in the classroom than earlier generations; however, they are skeptical about using their students' standardized test scores to measure such performance" (Coggshall, Ott, Behrstock, & Lasagna, 2010, p. 2).

"Performance pay plans that both get the best results and that employees prefer:

- Are based on fair measures related to performance;
- Reward all important goals of a job;
- Include frequent feedback on progress during the year;
- Provide substantial, motivating rewards for higher performance; and,
- Reward high-average, not just stellar, performers." (Hassel & Hassel, 2007, p. 10)

Focusing on Implementation Issues Involved With Shifting to a New Approach to Teacher Compensation

Robinson discussed differentiated pay plans for teachers during a previous period of interest in the approach. Based on the experiences of districts that had instituted—and most often abandoned—incentive pay plans, he suggests:

> To rush into a hastily constructed plan without giving proper attention to a school district's state of readiness, to its financial resources, and the importance of developing operational concepts and structures only increases the chances of failure and of reinforcing the belief that incentive pay for teachers is unworkable. (1984, p. 19)

Goldhaber also emphasizes the importance of careful planning by districts as they discuss and then move to a new approach to teacher compensation. In his view, the "devil is in the details," and he expresses concern about these. He expands on this:

> The broad discussion around reforming teacher pay tends to belie some of the complicated issues that arise when figuring out the practical details of how a given reform would actually work. It is easy, for instance, for policymakers to suggest that we ought to move away from a single salary schedule toward a [pay for performance]-based system, and in the abstract, this concept may make perfect sense. But do we know precisely how to structure rewards? Should they be individual or group-based? Should they cover teachers that are not in tested areas? In the case of individual-based plans, do we know how to judge the value-added of specific teachers? Do we know the appropriate size of incentives needed to induce the changes in teacher behavior that we might wish to see? Do school systems have the support infrastructures—adequate data, sufficient capacity in human resource and accounting departments, and so on—to implement and administer a new pay system? Were pay reform to be adopted, how would we know whether it was effective? I would argue that the answer to most of these questions is no for the vast majority of school systems. (2008, p. 16)

The Center for Educator Compensation Reform agrees about the complexity of the issues that need to be part of the conversation. To help districts in their efforts with designing and implementing systems, the Center has developed an "Implementation Checklist (download at http://www.cecr.ed.gov/pdfs/guide/CECRchecklist.pdf). For example, the following questions are just a few that should be addressed in the area of "Award Structure":

- Have you decided who will receive awards, such as individuals, groups, or both?
- If you intend to reward groups of teachers, have you determined which groups (e.g., all teachers in the school, all math teachers in the school, all 4th-grade math teachers in the school)?
- Do you fully understand the financial implications of individual and group awards to be offered?
- Have you decided whether the new compensation plan will be voluntary or mandatory?
- Have you decided whether the new compensation plan can be phased in as new teachers are hired or will it transfer all teachers to the new plan at the same time?
- Will current teachers be allowed to opt out if they want to remain under the present pay plan?
- Will the award structure be directly linked to desired teacher behaviors and student outcomes? (Excerpted from Center for Educator Compensation Reform, 2010, p. 5.)

"Ongoing and targeted communication between project leaders and stakeholder groups is critical to ensure programmatic success. Experience in districts' implementing performance-pay systems continues to show that securing teacher buy-in and commitment to a new compensation system is essential to a program's success as well as its long-term sustainability." (Koppich, Prince, Guthrie, & Schuermann, 2009, p. 1)

Ensuring the Necessary Funding Is—and Will Be—Available

Although funding for a new approach to teacher compensation is only one of the many issues that need to be addressed, it illustrates how complex a thoughtful planning process will need to be. Koppich, Prince, Guthrie, and Schuermann stress that the plan "must be affordable for the district, both now and into the future" (2009, p. 10). Heneman and Kimball see funding as a major stumbling block:

> Pursuit of a pay innovation without known and adequate funding is a hollow pursuit, and an innovation without funding guarantees will encounter serious launching and survival problems… Hence, funding requirements must be at the top of strategic issues to consider. Unfortunately, funding is invariably tight, and new funds for pay innovation can only come from internal reallocation or external infusion. (2008, p. 24)

The *structure* of the compensation system obviously has an impact on what the system in total will cost. The cost of some of these structural factors will be easier than others to project—for example, if particular categories of science teachers all receive a special increment to the salary schedule. Others are more difficult to estimate. For example, Hassel talks about performance-based awards:

> If all teachers can potentially win the maximum award, the potential liability is high. In private enterprises, companies can tie performance awards to the achievement of financial objectives; if many workers win performance awards, the company by design has the funds to make the payouts. Public education doesn't work that way. If an unexpectedly high number of teachers hit their targets, that does not mean the system has somehow garnered extra revenue to make the payments. But if there is a "fixed pot" for rewards, what will happen if the bonuses teachers qualify for exceed the funds available? Failure to follow through on promised awards can seriously undermine support for and the value of a performance-based system. (2002, p. 27)

Hassel and Hassel (2009) address the issue of incentive pay and talk about "internal reallocation" as the way to find the funds needed. Their analysis indicates that just 1% of the national "pie" that makes up teacher compensation is allocated to initiatives such as pay for National Board Certification, incentives to teach in hard-to-staff schools or subjects, and incentive pay, with the remainder going to base pay or pay tied to degree status or experience. They suggest that this pie be "re-sliced," with different approaches providing different levels of funding for the incentive programs:

- Small changes: If we wanted to give the top half of teachers performance bonuses averaging nearly $3,000 with top bonuses of over $6,000, we could by reducing post-5 year experience premiums by just 10% or by reducing advanced degree premiums by just 20%.
- Large changes: If we wanted to give the top 50% of teachers performance bonuses averaging $13,000 with the top teachers earning $20,000 (or more), we could by reducing post-5 year experience premiums by 50% or by reducing advanced degree premiums by 80%. (adapted from Hassel & Hassel, 2009)

Again, these possibilities represent more than simply shifts of dollars. There may be deeply held beliefs about the relevant merits or potential negative side effects of different approaches to compensating teachers that deserve to be heard in a thoughtful, comprehensive conversation.

References

Center for Educator Compensation Reform. (2010). *Implementation checklist—Guide to implementation: Resources for applied practice.* Retrieved from http://www.cecr.ed.gov/pdfs/guide/CECRchecklist.pdf

Center for Public Education. (2006). *Teacher quality and student achievement research review.* Retrieved from http://www.centerforpubliceducation.org/site/c.lvIXIiN0JWE/b.5057017/k.2A3C/Teacher_quality_and_student_achievement_research_review.htm

Center for Teaching Quality. (2006). *Teaching quality data systems roadmap*. Retrieved from http://www.teachingdata.org/

Chait, R., & Miller, R. (2009). *Paying teachers for results: A summary of research to inform the design of pay-for-performance programs for high-poverty schools.* Center for American Progress. Retrieved from http://www.americanprogress.org/issues/2009/05/pdf/performance_pay.pdf.

Coggshall, J. G., Ott, A., Behrstock, E., & Lasagna, M. (2010). *Retaining teacher talent: View from Generation Y*. Naperville, IL: Learning Point and New York: Public Agenda. Retrieved from http://www.learningpt.org/expertise/educatorquality/genY/SupportingTeacherEffectiveness/

Goldhaber, D. (2002, Spring). The mystery of good teaching. *Education Next*. Retrieved from http://www.educationnext.org/20021/50.html

Goldhaber, D. (2008). The politics of teacher pay reforms. Paper presented at 2008 national conference of the National Center on Performance Incentives. Retrieved from http://www.performanceincentives.org/data/files/directory/ConferencePapersNews/Goldhaber.pdf

Goldhaber, D. (2009). *Teacher pay reforms: The political implications of recent research.* Retrieved from http://www.americanprogress.org/issues/2006/12/pdf/teacher_pay_report.pdf.

Goldhaber, D., DeArmond, M., & DeBurgomaster, S. (2007). *Teacher attitudes about compensation reform: Implications for reform implementation.* School Finance Redesign Project, Center on Reinventing Public Education, University of Washington, Seattle, WA. Retrieved from http://www.nctq.org/nctq/research/1190908341618.pdf.

Hamilton, L., & Li, J. (2009). Designing effective pay-for-performance in K-12 education. Santa Monica, CA: RAND Education. Retrieved from http://www.rand.org/pubs/research_briefs/2009/RAND_RB9425.pdf

Harris Interactive. (2010). *The MetLife Survey of the American Teacher: Collaborating for student success—Part 1: Effective teaching and leadership.* New York: MetLife. Retrieved from http://www.metlife.com/assets/cao/contributions/foundation/american-teacher/MetLife_Teacher_Survey_2009_Part_1.pdf

Hassel, B. C. (2002). *Better pay for better teaching: Making teacher compensation pay off in the age of accountability.* Washington, DC: Progressive Policy Institute, 21st Century Schools Project. Retrieved from http://www.ppionline.org/documents/Hassel_May02.pdf

Hassel, B. C., & Hassel, E. A. (2009). *Re-slicing the teacher compensation pie: How to permanently fund teacher contributions to children's learning.* Retrieved from http://www.publicimpact.com/publications/Public_ImpactRe-SlicingtheTeacherCompensationPie.pdf

Hassel E. A., & Hassel, B. C. (2007). *Improving teaching through pay for contribution.* Washington, DC: NGA Center for Best Practices. Retrieved from http://www.nga.org/Files/pdf/0711IMPROVINGTEACHING.PDF

Heneman, H. G., & Kimball, S. (2008). *How to design new teacher salary structures. Consortium for Policy Research in Education Policy Briefs.* Retrieved from http://www.smhc-cpre.org

Heneman, H. G., Milanowski, A., & Kimball, S. (2007). *Teacher performance pay: Synthesis of plans, research, and guidelines for practice.* Strategic Management of Human Capital, Consortium for Policy Research in Education. Retrieved from http://www.cpre.org/images/stories/cpre_pdfs/RB46.pdf.

Heyburn, S., Lewis, J., & Ritter, G. (2010). Compensation reform and design preferences of Teacher Incentive Fund grantees. Nashville, TN: National Center on Performance Incentives. Retrieved from http://www.performanceincentives.org/data/files/news/PapersNews/Heyburn_et_al_2010.pdf.

Honawar, V. (2009). Performance pay studies show few achievement gains. *Education Week.* Retrieved from http://www.edweek.org/ew/articles/2008/03/12/27pay.h27.html.

Koppich, J. E., Prince, C. D., Guthrie, J. W., & Schuermann, P. J. (2009). Stakeholder engagement and communication: Guide to implementation—Resources for applied practice. Washington, DC: Center for Educator Compensation Reform, U.S. Department of Education. Retrieved from http://www.cecr.ed.gov/guides/CECRStakeholderEngagement.pdf

Lavy, V. (2007, Spring). Using performance-based pay to improve the quality of teachers. *Future of Children,* 87-109. Retrieved from http://www.eric.ed.gov/ERICDocs/data/ericdocs2sql/content_storage_01/0000019b/80/3d/d6/0b.pdf

Learning Point Associates. (2007, June). Improving teacher retention with supportive workplace conditions. *Newsletter.* Washington, DC: The Center for Comprehensive School Reform and Improvement. Retrieved from http://www.centerforcsri.org/files/TheCenter_NL_June07.pdf

National Commission on Teaching and America's Future. (2003). *No dream denied: A pledge to America's children* (Summary report). Washington, DC: Author. Retrieved from http://www.nctaf.org/documents/no-dream-denied_summary_report.pdf

Odden, A. (2000). *Seven reasons to change teacher compensation*. Madison, WI: Consortium for Policy Research in Education. Retrieved from http://cpre.wceruw.org/tcomp/general/sevenreasons.php

Robinson, G.E. (1984, March). *Concerns in education: Incentive pay for teachers: An analysis of approaches*. Arlington, VA: Educational Research Service.

Scholastic and the Bill & Melinda Gates Foundation. (2010). Primary sources: America's teachers on America's schools. Retrieved from http://www.scholastic.com/primarysources/pdfs/Scholastic_Gates_noapp_0310.pdf

U.S. Department of Education. (2010). Teacher Incentive Fund: Summary of notice of proposed priorities. Retrieved from http://www2.ed.gov/programs/teacherincentive/applicant.html